LIVE BEAT 3

WORKBOOK

T0345700

Rod Fricker

Contents

a

Vocabulary: Personality adjectives

1 ⭐ **Match the sentences (1–6) to the personality words (a–f).**

1 Debbie borrows my clothes without asking and spends ages in the bathroom. She's really … c

2 Mark is always angry. I don't know why he's so … ___

3 Louise is always first in tests and knows all the answers in lessons. She's really … ___

4 Paula always makes us laugh. She's very … ___

5 Tom is always willing to do jobs around the house. He's very … ___

6 Donna's nice but she doesn't say much. She's very … ___

a) funny. d) helpful.
b) quiet. e) bad-tempered.
c) annoying. f) clever.

2 ⭐⭐ **Complete the sentences with the correct personality adjectives.**

1 Frank always says hello and smiles when he meets you. He's very f*riendly*.

2 Belinda always tells people what to do. She's very b_____.

3 Ed never worries about anything and never gets nervous. He's very e_____ -g_____.

4 Gina shares everything with her friends, she even gives away her last sweets. She's very g_____.

5 Liam never does anything. He doesn't do housework and he hates doing exercise. He's very l_____.

6 Rob never says hello or please or thank you. He's very r_____.

7 Sue finds it difficult to talk to people she doesn't know. She's quite s_____.

8 Ursula's room is always a mess. She's very u_____.

Grammar: Present simple and present continuous

3 ⭐ **Match the questions (1–7) to the answers (a–g).**

1 What are you doing? _d_
2 Are you using this pen? ___
3 What's the weather like today? ___
4 What does your dad do? ___
5 Do you know that girl's name? ___
6 What are you studying in History? ___
7 What do you want to do this weekend? ___

a) No, I'm not. You can borrow it if you want.
b) I'd like to go to the cinema.
c) No, I don't. I think she's new.
d) I'm reading a book.
e) It's raining.
f) We're learning about Henry VIII.
g) He's a teacher.

4 ⭐⭐ **Use the prompts to complete the dialogue.**

A: Hi, Mark. ¹*Do you remember* (you remember) me?

B: … er, Sara?

A: That's right. It's great to see you. ²_____ (What/you/do) here?

B: ³_____ (I/wait) for a bus.

A: Yes, but ⁴_____ (where/you/go)?

B: Oh, sorry. ⁵_____ (I/go) to the sports centre. My brother's there. ⁶_____ (He/play) badminton every Saturday.

A: ⁷_____ (you/like) sports?

B: Not really. ⁸_____ (I/prefer) shopping.

A: Me too.

B: ⁹_____ (you/go) shopping now?

A: Yes. Oh look. ¹⁰_____ (The bus/come).

B: Maybe I can meet you later?

A: Yes, that's a great idea. Here's my phone number ….

4

b

Vocabulary: House and furniture

1 ★ **Label the picture. Complete the text with the objects (1–6).**

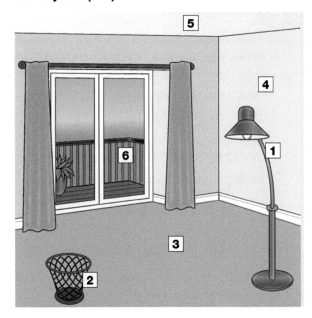

This is my new room. There isn't any furniture in it at the moment. There's just a ¹*lamp* and a ² _____ on the ³ _____. I want to paint the ⁴ _____ green and the ⁵ _____ blue, like the sky. That will look cool. The best thing about my room is that it's got a ⁶ _____. I do my homework there when it's warm.

2 ★★ **Complete the words.**

1 You wash in the b*athroom*.

2 You put your books in the b_____.

3 You keep your clothes in your w_____.

4 You put a c_____ on the floor to walk on.

5 If you have a d_____, you don't need to do the washing-up.

6 My sister always looks at herself in the m_____ before she goes out.

7 In our house, the bedrooms and bathroom are u_____ and the kitchen and living room are d_____.

8 You wash your hands in a w_____, but dishes and pots in the s_____.

9 The f_____ keeps your food cold.

10 We keep the car in the g_____ at night.

Grammar: Countable and uncountable nouns with *some, any, a/an* and *no*

3 ★ **Choose the correct options.**

1 There aren't ___ stairs in this house.
   a) any   b) no   c) some

2 Is there ___ mirror in your bedroom?
   a) some   b) a   c) any

3 Great! We haven't got ___ homework this weekend.
   a) some   b) any   c) no

4 It's Monday, but there's ___ school because it's a holiday.
   a) no   b) any   c) a

5 There are ___ interesting photos in this album.
   a) any   b) a   c) some

6 We live in a flat so we haven't got ___ garden.
   a) a   b) no   c) any

7 Why are there ___ books in your bookcase?
   a) any   b) a)   c) no

8 We've got ___ nice, old house.
   a) some   b) a   c) an

4 ★★ **Complete the dialogue with *a, an, any, some* or *no*.**

Adam: I need to make my bedroom look nice.

Lisa: You could put ¹*some* posters on your walls.

Adam: I haven't got ² _____ posters. No, what I want is ³ _____ plant. ⁴ _____ interesting, colourful and very big plant. The problem is there are ⁵ _____ plant shops near my house.

Lisa: Really? None at all? The garden centre on Park Road is good. They've got ⁶ _____ beautiful plants there.

Adam: OK, good idea. Thanks. My mum can take me on Saturday.

Lisa: Can I come? I can help you choose ⁷ _____ nice plants.

Adam: Thanks! I could use ⁸ _____ help.

WELCOME

Vocabulary: Jobs

1 ⭐ **Match the word beginnings (1–5 and 6–10) to the endings (a–e and f–j) to make jobs.**

1 wait	a) el
2 act	b) ist
3 art	c) er
4 electric	d) or
5 mod	e) ian
6 secret	f) ant
7 doct	g) ian
8 shop assist	h) ress
9 wait	i) ary
10 music	j) or

2 ⭐ **Look at the pictures and complete the jobs with one letter in each space.**

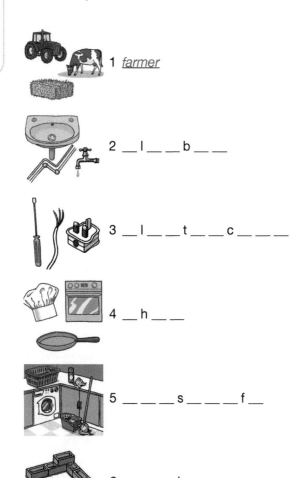

1 *farmer*

2 __ l __ __ b __ __ __

3 __ l __ __ t __ __ c __ __ __ __

4 __ h __ __ __

5 __ __ __ s __ __ __ f __

6 __ __ __ l __ __ r

Grammar: Past simple and past continuous; Time markers: *when, while*

3 ⭐ **Complete the text with the phrases from the box.**

- while I was working • When I finished
- while I was taking • While I was giving
- the actress was walking
- while he was standing

One day last summer, ¹*while I was working* as a waiter, a famous actress walked in. I took her to her table. A bit later, she called to me ² _____ plates of food to another table. I couldn't suddenly stop so I carried on working. ³ _____ the customers their food, I suddenly realised that the actress was standing right behind me. 'I'm waiting,' she said, angrily. I told her that I was busy and turned away. ⁴ _____ serving the other customers, I turned around and saw that ⁵ _____ out of the restaurant. My boss was very angry at first but, ⁶ _____ there, looking at me, all the other customers started clapping and cheering. My boss realised that I was right and she was wrong. I never liked her films anyway!

4 ⭐⭐ **Complete the second sentence so that it has the same meaning as the first.**

1 While I was walking to school, it started to rain.

   I was *walking to school when it started to rain.*

2 I was playing computer games when the electricity went off.

   The electricity _____.

3 The police officer was driving when he saw the bank robbers.

   While the _____.

d

Grammar: *Wh-* questions; Question words

1 ⭐ **Choose the correct options.**

1 '___ dress do you want?' 'The blue one.'

   a) What   b) Which   c) How

2 '___ did you get those shoes?' 'In the new shop in town.'

   a) How much   b) Where   c) How long

3 '___ were they?' '£24.99.'

   a) How many   b) How much   c) How far

4 '___ are these trainers?' 'They're John's.'

   a) Who   b) Where   c) Whose

5 '___ pairs of shoes have you got?' 'About 15.'

   a) How long   b) How much   c) How many

6 '___ do you go shopping for clothes?' 'Every Saturday.'

   a) How often   b) How long   c) How far

7 '___ do you like this shop?' 'It's very cheap.'

   a) Why   b) Which   c) Where

8 '___ gave you this shirt?' 'My aunt.'

   a) What   b) Who   c) Whose

2 ⭐⭐ **Complete the questions.**

A: Excuse me. ¹*What* do you do?

B: I'm a teacher.

A: ² _____ do you work?

B: At St Mark's School in Coventry.

A: ³ _____ away is that?

B: It's about 6 km from here.

A: ⁴ _____ do you get to work?

B: By car.

A: ⁵ _____ of car have you got?

B: A Nissan Micra.

A: ⁶ _____ are your students?

B: They're aged from eleven to eighteen.

A: ⁷ _____ students are there in the school?

B: About 1,200.

A: ⁸ _____ do you give homework?

B: Once a week.

Vocabulary: Clothes

3 ⭐ **Look at the picture and match the words (1–11) to the numbers (1–4).**

1 T-shirt	*3*	7 plain	___
2 jumper	___	8 patterned	___
3 gloves	___	9 striped	___
4 dress	___	10 tight	___
5 sleeveless	___	11 spotted	___
6 baggy	___		

4 ⭐⭐ **Label the picture.**

1 baseball cap

2 s_____

3 c_____
  s_____

4 b_____

5 p_____

6 z_____

7 j_____

8 s_____

9 s_____

1a I'm going to apply.

Vocabulary: Types of music and musical instruments

1 ⭐ **Rearrange the letters to make types of music.**

MUSIC FESTIVAL
This weekend in the park

Music from all over the world.

We have ¹*jazz* (zajz), ²_____ (nalit), ³_____ (areegg), ⁴_____ (luso), ⁵_____ (chonte), ⁶_____ (slacislac), ⁷_____ (cork), ⁸_____ (vahye talem), and, from the USA, ⁹_____ (troncyu) and _____ (stewner).

It's free so come and have fun in the sun!

2 ⭐⭐ **Label the picture.**

1 c*ello*   6 t_____

2 d_____   7 c_____

  b_____   8 f_____

3 v_____   9 s_____

4 g_____   10 k_____

5 d_____

Grammar: Future with *going to* and *will*

3 ⭐ **Match the functions from the box to the sentences.**

- plan   • ~~intention~~   • promise
- prediction with evidence
- prediction without evidence   • decision

1 I'm going to work harder next year.   *intention*

2 I don't know this film, but I think you'll enjoy it.   _____

3 'There are three tickets left for the concert.' 'Oh, I'll have one.'   _____

4 This film is brilliant. It's going to win lots of Oscars.   _____

5 I'll give you back your DVD next week.
_____

6 We're going to leave at eight o'clock tomorrow morning.   _____

4 ⭐⭐ **Complete the sentences with the best form of the words in brackets.**

Tara: Where ¹*will we be* (we/be) in twenty years' time?

Gina: I've no idea.

Tara: I think ²_____ (you/have) your own business. ³_____ (You/be) a photographer or an artist or something like that. ⁴_____ (You/not/be) rich, but ⁵_____ (you/be) very happy.

Gina: Well, I know something. ⁶_____ (I/not/pass) the Maths exam tomorrow. I don't understand it at all!

5 ★★★ Complete the dialogue with the correct form of the verbs from the box.

- ~~start~~ • call • think • make • put
- not get • be • not do

Steve: Hi, Gerry. How are your guitar lessons?

Gerry: Great. I'm quite good now. I ¹*'m going to start* a band.

Steve: Really? Do you know any other musicians?

Gerry: No, but I've got this advert. I ²_____ it on the noticeboard at the music school when I go for my lesson this afternoon.

Steve: Good idea! Hey, I know. I ³_____ your manager. I ⁴_____ you famous but you have to promise me something.

Gerry: What?

Steve: That you ⁵_____ a different manager if you become successful. You know, some big name from the USA.

Gerry: Don't worry! I ⁶_____ anything to upset you. You're my best friend.

Steve: Hey. What ⁷_____ your band? You need a good name.

Gerry: I haven't thought about it. I guess I ⁸_____ of a name when I know who the other members are. Right, I must go. My lesson starts soon.

Steve: OK, see you later.

Grammar summary

Future with *going to*

Affirmative	Negative
I**'m going to work** hard.	I**'m not going to work** hard.
You**'re going to be** late.	You **aren't going to be** late.
He/She/It**'s going to win**.	He/She/It **isn't going to win**.
We**'re going to watch** a film.	We **aren't going to watch** a film.
Questions	**Short answers**
Are you **going to finish** soon?	Yes, I **am**.
Am I **going to be** in the team?	No, I**'m not**.
Is he/she/it **going to wait** for us?	Yes, you **are**.
Are we/they **going to leave** soon?	No, you **aren't**.
	Yes, he/she/it **is**.
	No, he/she/it **isn't**.
	Yes, we/they **are**.
	No, we/they **aren't**.

Note

Use

We use *going to* for plans, intentions and predictions based on present evidence.

Form

We use the correct form of the verb *to be* + *going to* + infinitive without *to*.

Future with *will*

Affirmative
I/You/He/She/It/We/They**'ll (will) be** successful.

Negative
I/You/He/She/It/We/They **won't (will not) live** here in the future.

Questions
Will I/you/he/she/it/we/they **be** rich in the future?

Short answers
Yes, I/you/he/she/it/we/they **will**.
No, I/you/he/she/it/we/they **won't (will not)**.

Note

Use

We use *will* for decisions made at the time of speaking, promises and predictions made without present evidence.

Form

We use *will* + infinitive without *to*. We don't need any other auxiliary verb to make questions and negatives.

1b I'm going out.

Phrases

1 ⭐ Complete the dialogue with the phrases from the box.

> • can make it • can't make it • hang on
> • ~~What's up?~~

Jane: Hello, Sally.

Sally: Hi, Jane. ¹*What's up?*

Jane: It's Ruth. She ² _____ on Friday evening. She's looking after her little sister. We'll have to meet on Saturday.

Sally: OK. No, ³ _____ a minute. Saturday's no good for me. I'm going out with Harry. Friday's the only day that I ⁴ _____. Why don't we meet at Ruth's on Friday? We can all look after her little sister.

Jane: That's a good idea!

Grammar: Present continuous for future arrangements

2 ⭐ Complete the sentences with the correct form of the verbs in brackets.

1 *I'm going* (I/go) to the dentist on Tuesday afternoon.

2 _____ (Simon/meet) his friend Julie on Wednesday.

3 _____ (Tom and I/play) tennis later today.

4 _____ (My mum and dad/ have) a party on Friday.

5 _____ (What/you/do) after school today?

6 _____ (We/not go) on a school trip this month.

7 _____ (you/work) on Friday evening?

8 _____ (I/get) a new computer for my birthday next month.

3 ⭐⭐ Use the prompts to complete the dialogues.

1

A: I'm in the school play.

B: Really? You/play/Romeo?
   Are you playing Romeo?

A: No/not. I/play/the Prince.

   _____

B: Who/play/Romeo?

   _____

A: Nick Parker.

2

A: you/meet/Simon this weekend?

   _____

B: Yes/I/. We/go/to the cinema.

   _____

A: he/take/you out for dinner as well?

   _____

B: No/not. He/come/to my house for dinner.

   _____

3

A: you/do/anything tomorrow?

   _____

B: No, I/not. Why?

   _____

A: I/meet/Kate at Pizza Palace.

   _____

B: So?

A: She/bring/her friend, Theresa.

   _____

B: Oh, right. Great, I'll be there.

Use your English: Make arrangements: invite, accept, refuse (with excuses)

4 ★ **Choose the correct options.**

1 Would you ___ to go out on Friday?

  a) want   b) like   c) fancy

2 ___ you want to go for a picnic?

  a) Would)   b) What about   c) Do

3 Do you fancy ___ for a swim later?

  a) going   b) go   c) to go

4 I'd ___ to come.

  a) fancy   b) want   c) love

5 Thanks ___ asking.

  a) for   b) with   c) from

6 'How about having a party?' 'Yes, that ___ great.'

  a) looks   b) would   c) sounds

7 'Do you want to go out later?' 'No, I don't really ___ it, thanks.'

  a) want   b) fancy   c) like

5 ★★ **Complete the dialogues with the words and phrases from the box.**

- What about • I can't • ~~Would you~~
- I'm afraid • Do you • I'd love (x 2)
- sounds great • for asking • fancy going

1 **Simon:** Hi, Matt. Hi Dave. ¹*Would you* like to come to my party on Friday?

  Matt: Sure, ²_____ to.

  Dave: Thanks ³_____, but I don't think I can.

2 **Charles:** ⁴_____ want to see a film tonight?

  Anna: Sorry, ⁵_____. I'm meeting Helen.

3 **Paul:** Do you ⁶_____ to a concert tomorrow?

  Sam: Yes, that ⁷_____.

  Tina: ⁸_____ I can't. We're going to my aunt's house.

4 **Lisa:** ⁹_____ meeting in the park later?

  Donna: ¹⁰_____ to, but I've got lots of homework.

Grammar summary

Present continuous for future arrangements

Affirmative

I**'m meeting** Tom later.
You**'re playing** at six o'clock.
He**'s coming** later.
She**'s working** this evening.
We**'re meeting** outside the theatre.
They**'re staying** for dinner.

Negative

I**'m not meeting** Tom tonight.
You **aren't playing** in this competition.
He **isn't coming** until tomorrow.
She **isn't going out** this evening.
We **aren't having** a test tomorrow.
They **aren't staying** for the night.

Questions	Short answers
Are you **meeting** Chris?	Yes, I **am**. / No, I**'m not**.
Am I **playing** today?	Yes, you **are**.
	No, you **aren't**.
Is he **flying** to Paris tomorrow?	Yes, he **is**.
	No, he **isn't**.
Is she **having** a party next week?	Yes, she **is**.
	No, she **isn't**.
Are we **getting** the bus to Gran's?	Yes, we **are**.
	No, we **aren't**.
Are they **going** anywhere tonight?	Yes, they **are**.
	No, they **aren't**.

Note

Use

- We use the present continuous for future arrangements and fixed plans.
  I'm meeting Simon.
- We often use time adverbials like *next week, at the weekend, later* to show that the activity is in the future.
  I'm going to my aunt's this weekend.

Form

- We use the correct form of the verb *to be* + *verb* + *ing*. The form is exactly the same as the present continuous for things happening now.

Common mistakes

- We can't use the present continuous to make future predictions.
  ~~It's raining soon.~~ ✗
  It's going to rain soon. ✓

1c They're the best films ever!

Vocabulary: Adjectives of opinion

1 ⭐ **Choose the correct options.**

1 I didn't really understand the film because it was very ___.
   a) violent   b) confusing

2 What a great horror film. It was really ___!
   a) scary   b) funny

3 I can't believe this film is for twelve-year-olds. It's much too ___.
   a) violent   b) sad

4 It was really ___. I couldn't stop laughing.
   a) complicated   b) funny

5 It was so ___ when the hero died. I cried and cried.
   a) confusing   b) sad

6 It was a good horror film and the music made it even more ___.
   a) frightening   b) violent

7 You have to watch very carefully because it's quite a ___ story.
   a) scary   b) complicated

2 ⭐⭐ **Complete the adjectives.**

The film was very good.
It was …
1 a m a z i n g
2 _ w _ s _ _ _
3 _ x _ _ l _ _ n _
4 _ x _ _ t _ _ _
5 _ _ j _ y _ _ _ e
6 _ _ t _ _ _ s _ _ _ g

The film was very bad.
It was …
7 _ w _ u _
8 _ o _ _ _ g
9 _ _ s _ p _ _ _ _ t _ _ _
10 _ u _ l

Grammar: Comparison of adjectives *much* + comparative adjective *(not) as … as*; Superlatives

3 ⭐ **Complete the sentences with the words from the box.**

> • sad • more • isn't • worse • as • ~~than~~
> • much • the • worst

1 Can we watch the film on Channel 2? It's better *than* this one.

2 What a terrible film. It was _____ than doing my homework!

3 Mum. Can I watch *The Ring*? It isn't _____ scary as *The Grudge*!

4 The _____ film I saw on television last year was *The Avengers*.

5 European films are _____ interesting than American ones.

6 I think Daniel Day Lewis is _____ best actor in the world.

7 The film wasn't as _____ as I was expecting.

8 Jim Carrey is funny, but he _____ as funny as Ben Stiller.

9 I think films now are _____ more scary than when we were young.

4 ⭐⭐ **Complete text with the correct form of the adjectives in brackets. Add any other words necessary.**

James Bond films are now more than fifty years old. But which one is ¹*the best* (good) and who is your favourite Bond? Here's what we found out.

²_____ (good) Bond is Sean Connery but ³_____ (exciting) film is *Skyfall*. Sean Connery's best film was *Goldfinger*, but it isn't ⁴_____ (good) as any of the Daniel Craig films. ⁵_____ (scary) baddie was Baron Samedi in *Live and Let Die*.

The new Bond films are ⁶_____ (exciting) the old films. That's what most young people think. They say that the old films were

7_____ (dull) the new ones but older

people don't think the new films are 8_____

(enjoyable) as the old ones.

What about Bond songs? Some of you said that

Adele's *Skyfall* was amazing but others say it

was 9_____ (dull) of all the Bond songs.

Your favourite Bond singer is Shirley Bassey. She

sang two songs and you said that *Goldfinger* was

10_____ (good) *Diamonds Are Forever*.

5 ★★★ **Use the prompts and the information in the table to write sentences.**

Old or New?

Star Wars	Exciting	Enjoyable
Old	★★★	★★★★★
New	★★★★	★★★

1 The old Star Wars films/not/exciting/new Star Wars films

The old Star Wars films aren't as exciting as the new Star Wars films.

2 The old Star Wars films/much/enjoyable/new

_____

3 good/film/is/the first one

_____

4 bad/film/is/the fifth one

_____

Ocean's Eleven	Acting	How cool is it?
Old	★★	★★★★
New	★★★	★★★★

5 The acting in the old film/not/good/the acting in the new film

_____

6 The actors in the original film/cool/the actors in the new film

_____

7 They not/good-looking/George Clooney and Brad Pitt though!

_____

Grammar summary

Comparison of adjectives

Comparatives and superlatives

Regular short adjectives

New York is **(much) bigger** than London.
DVD's are (aren't) **as good as** films in the cinema.
Slender Man is **the scariest** game on the internet.

Regular long adjectives

Horror films are **more frightening** than computer games.
Normal films are (aren't) **as enjoyable as** 3D films.
My brother is **the most annoying** person I know.

Irregular adjectives

Skyfall is **(much) better** than *Casino Royale*.
Anne Hathaway is **the best young** actress in Hollywood.
The film is **(much) worse** than the book.
Surfing the Net is **the worst** way to spend the evening.

Note

Use

- We use comparatives + *than* to compare two things.
  Matt Damon is younger than Robert De Niro.
- We use *as* + adjective + *as* to say that two things are the same and *not as* + adjective + *as* to say that two things are different.
  Playing football is (not) as enjoyable as playing tennis.
- We use superlatives to compare more than two people or things.
  I'm the tallest girl in my class.

Spelling rules

After one syllable adjectives:

- We usually add *-er/-est*.
  young – younger/youngest
- After *-e*, we add *-r/-st*
  nice – nicer/nicest
- After one vowel and one consonant, we double the final consonant and add *-er/-est*.
  big – bigger/biggest

For two or more syllable adjectives:

- We usually use *more/most* + adjective.
  interesting – more/most interesting
- After two syllable adjectives ending in *-y*, we change the *-y* to *-i* and add *-er/-est*.
  pretty – prettier/prettiest

Common mistakes

~~Sue isn't so nice like Jane.~~ ✗
Sue isn't as nice as Jane. ✓
~~Beth is more older than Mandy.~~ ✗
Beth is older than Mandy. ✓

1 Put the words in the box into the correct spaces.

• cello • violin • awesome • techno • dull
• awful • clarinet • enjoyable • classical
• flute • jazz

What instrument did you play?

1 cello _____ _____ _____

What kind of music did they play?

2 _____ _____ _____

What did you think of the concert? (It was great.)

3 _____ _____

What do you think of the CD? (It's bad.)

4 _____ _____

.../10

2 Use the prompts to write questions and answers.

1 A: you/want/come/to a concert tonight?

B: Yes/I/come

A: Do you want to come to a concert tonight?

B: Yes, I'll come.

2 A: When/you/do/your homework?

B: Er./I/do/it after this film, I promise.

_____

_____

3 A: When/you/meet/Amy?

B: I/meet/her tomorrow at eleven o'clock

_____

_____

4 A: you/fancy/go/to the cinema tonight?

B: I/can't. We/go/to my grandmother's tonight

_____

_____

5 A: you/like/come/to my party on Saturday?

B: afraid/can't but/thanks/ask

_____

_____

6 A: you/still/live here in ten years' time?

B: No/not. It's boring here.

_____

_____

.../10

3 Complete the dialogue with the correct form of the words in brackets.

A: The ¹best (good) thing about *Life of Pi* was the 3D effects. They were ² _____ (good) than in *Avatar*.

B: No way. They weren't as ³ _____ (good) as *Avatar*. That was brilliant.

A: Do you want to see *Avatar 2*?

B: No. Second films are always ⁴ _____ (bad) than originals.

A: Not always. *Madagascar 2* was ⁵ _____ (funny) than *Madagascar 1* and *Pirates of the Caribbean 2* was ⁶ _____ (enjoyable) than the first film.

B: You're joking! *Pirates of the Caribbean 2* was the ⁷ _____ (complicated) film ever and it was the ⁸ _____ (bad) of the four films.

A: Yeah, it wasn't as ⁹ _____ (interesting) as the other films but Penelope Cruz is the ¹⁰ _____ (beautiful) actress in Hollywood.

B: And the ¹¹ _____ (scary)!

.../10

4 Complete the second sentence so that it has the same meaning as the first.

1 Stephen isn't as old as me.

Stephen is *younger than* me.

2 My plan is to get a summer job this year.

I'm _____ this year.

3 I've arranged to visit my cousin on Friday.

I'm _____ on Friday.

4 No actor is better than Robert De Niro!

Robert De Niro _____ in the world!

5 Rap isn't better than techno and it isn't worse.

Rap is _____ techno.

6 French is difficult, but German is very difficult.

German is _____ French.

.../10

🎧 **LISTEN AND CHECK YOUR SCORE**

Total	.../40

1 Skills practice

SKILLS FOCUS: READING AND WRITING

Read

1 **Read about a music festival and match the headings (1–3) to the paragraphs (A–C).**

1 Lots of things to do

2 See your work at the festival

3 See interesting and famous people

 SOUNDTRACK FESTIVAL

| Home | News | Music | About | Sign up |

A *1*
The Soundtrack Festival started in 2008. I read about it on the internet and decided to go. It was brilliant. As well as watching films, I listened to film makers talking about their work, watched musicians and bands in concert and learned how to turn a book into a film.

B ___
I went to the festival a few years ago. There were a lot of interesting people there. I know it doesn't attract Oscar winning actors or directors but I didn't mind that. When I was there, I saw the rock band Gong, composers, film producers, poets and the musician, John Cale.

C ___
I really enjoyed watching films by unknown film makers. Some of them were full-length movies and others were short films. They were as good as the films they showed made by more famous film makers. Anyone can send a film to the festival and they show the best. It's completely free. I'm going to try next year.

2 **Read the text again and answer true (T), false (F) or doesn't say (DS).**

1 At the festival, you can listen to music. *T*

2 At the festival, you can meet Oscar winning actors. ___

3 'Gong' is the title of a film. ___

4 The full-length films were better than the short films. ___

5 The festival doesn't show all the films people send to it. ___

Write

3 **Complete the email with the words from the box.**

- Hi • going • Bye • How's • Do (x 2)
- now • fancy • want

[1]Hi Rebecca,

[2]_____ it [3]_____? I hope you enjoyed the concert last night.
I'm meeting Ben and Josh at Burger City this afternoon. We're meeting at three o'clock. I know the food isn't great, but it's cheaper than other places. [4]_____ you [5]_____ meeting us there?
After lunch, I'm going to go shopping. I need to buy some new shoes. [6]_____ you [7]_____ to come with me? You're always good at choosing clothes.
I hope you can come. It'll be lovely to see you and you can tell me all about the concert.
[8]_____ for [9]_____.

Vicky

4 **Use the notes to write a reply to Vicky.**

- Greeting: Thank Vicky for the email. Tell her your opinion of the concert.

- Main message: Tell Vicky you can't meet for lunch – your aunt is coming for dinner – you would like to meet later and go shopping – you need to buy clothes, too.

- Details and arrangements: Arrange when and where to meet. Suggest something to do after shopping.

- Summary and conclusion: Thank Vicky again. Tell her you hope she has a nice lunch.

2a I've just told you.

Vocabulary: Household jobs

1 ★ **Complete the puzzle.**

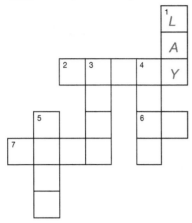

1 _lay_ the table
2 _____ the dishwasher
3 _____ the breakfast
4 _____ your room
5 _____ the car
6 _____ the cleaning
7 _____ the rubbish out

2 ★ **Look at the pictures and complete the jobs.**

1

_do_ the _vacuuming_

2

_____ the _____

3

_____ the _____

4

_____ the _____

5

_____ the _____

6

_____ the _____

7

_____ the _____

Grammar: Present perfect simple with time adverbials *ever, never, already, just, yet*

3 ★ **Choose the correct responses.**

1 You look tired.
   a) Yes, I've already tidied my room.
   b) Yes, I've just tidied my room.

2 Do your homework!
   a) I haven't done it yet.
   b) I've already done it.

3 Have you ever lost something important?
   a) No, never.   b) No, not yet.

4 Your hair looks different today.
   a) Yes, I've had it cut.
   b) Yes, I've already had it cut.

5 Have you done the washing-up yet?
   a) No, I've already walked in the door.
   b) No, I've just walked in the door.

6 Why don't you want to see the film?
   a) I've already seen it.   b) I've never seen it.

4 ★★ **Use the prompts to write questions and answers.**

1 A: you/ever/see/the Eiffel Tower?
   B: ✓. I/be/to the top twice.
   A: Have you ever seen the Eiffel Tower?
   B: Yes, I have. I've been to the top twice.

2 A: you/tidy/your room yet?
   B: I/start/but/I not finish/yet

   _____

   _____

3 A: you/ever/find/money in the street?
   B: ✗. but I/lose/lots of money!

   _____

   _____

4 A: Jack/do/the washing-up yet?
   B: ✓. and/he/already/empty/the dishwasher

   _____

   _____

5 ★★★ **Complete the dialogues with the prompts from the box.**

- Yes, just/buy • I/never/be/there • I/never/make • ~~No/already/see~~ • No, not/finish/yet

1

A: Do you want to watch this DVD?

B: *No, I've already seen it.*

2
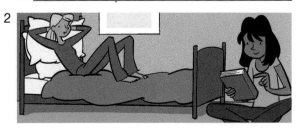

A: Can I borrow this book?

B: _____

3

A: Is that shirt new?

B: _____

4

A: Do you like New York?

B: _____

5

A: So, how do we make a cake?

B: I don't know. _____

Grammar summary

Present perfect simple with time adverbials *ever, never, already, just, yet*
Present perfect simple with *just* and *already*
I**'ve just finished** my homework.
He**'s already gone** out.
Present perfect simple with *yet*
Have they **arrived yet?**
She **hasn't woken up yet**.
Present perfect simple with *ever* and *never*
Have you **ever been** to Venice?
Has he **ever forgotten** your birthday?
We**'ve never been** late to school.
She**'s never eaten** Chinese food.

Note

Use

- We use the present perfect simple with *just* to say that something happened a very short time ago.
  I'm tired because I've just woken up.
- We use *already* to emphasise that something has happened before now.
  We've already done this exercise!
- We use *yet* in negative sentences and questions to mean *up to now*.
  I haven't done the washing-up yet (but I will do it).
  Have you tidied your room yet?
- We use *never* to mean *at no time in my life*.
  I have never failed an exam.
- We use *ever* in questions to mean *at any time in your life*.
  Have you ever had a summer job?

Form

- We put *just*, *already*, *ever* and *never* before the main verb.
  *I have **never cooked** dinner.*
  *We have **just finished** our exam.*
  *They have **already left**.*
  *Have you **ever seen** a famous person?*
- We put *yet* at the end of negative sentences and questions.
  *Have you finished **yet**?*
  *He hasn't sent me an email **yet**.*

Common mistakes

~~I haven't never been to Rome.~~ ✗
I've never been to Rome. ✓
~~Have you done your homework already?~~ ✗
Have you done your homework yet? ✓

2b He asked me out.

Vocabulary: Relationship words and phrases

1 ⭐ **Complete the sentences with one word in each space.**

1 I'm really annoyed _with_ my brother. He's taken my MP3 player without asking.

2 I had an argument _____ Tom and now I'm really upset.

3 Hi, you're new here, aren't you? Do you want to _____ friends with us?

4 Julie started going _____ with Chris when they were in Year 11.

5 Did you fall _____ with Luke because he forgot your birthday?

6 I get _____ well with most of the people in my class.

7 My friend's parents are going to _____ divorced and she's really sad.

8 Peter asked me _____ on a date. Do you think I should say 'Yes'?

9 I was really angry with Rob, but he said sorry and now we've made _____.

2 ⭐⭐ **Look at the pictures and complete the phrases with one word in each space.**

1 John and Emily met at a party and immediately f_ell_ in l_ove_ w_ith_ each other.

2 Emily b_____ u_____ w_____ John after an argument, but they soon got back together.

3 John g_____ e_____ t_____ Emily in a restaurant when they were both twenty-two years old.

4 John g_____ m_____ t_____ Emily in 2012.

Grammar: Present perfect simple and past simple; Time adverbials

3 ⭐⭐ **Complete the sentences with one of the verbs in brackets in the past simple and the other in the present perfect.**

1 I _met_ (meet) Eric three weeks ago.
My parents _have just met_ (just meet) Eric.

2 I _____ (do) my homework last night.
I _____ (already do) my homework.

3 I _____ (never be) in a school play.
I _____ (not be) in the school play last year.

4 _____ (you ever go) to Greece?
_____ (you go) to Greece last summer?

4 ⭐⭐⭐ **Use the prompts to write questions and sentences.**

1 A: you/do/the washing-up yet?
B: ✓. I/do/it this morning.
A: Have you done the washing-up yet?
B: Yes, I have. I did it this morning.

2 A: When you/go to ask/Melanie/out?
B: I/already/ask/her. I/ask/her yesterday.
A: _____
B: _____

3 A: you/ever/be/in love?
B: ✓. I/fall/in love last night.
A: _____
B: _____

4 A: I/never/have/an argument with my sister.
B: Yes, you have. You/have/one last week
A: _____
B: _____

Use your English: Talk about problems: suggestions and advice

5 ★ **Complete the sentences with one word in each space.**

1 I don't k<u>now</u> what to do about my annoying brother.

2 I'm a b_____ worried about my schoolwork.

3 What's the m_____?

4 M_____ you should eat less junk food.

5 W_____ don't you ask your parents for advice?

6 You look f_____ u_____.

7 I don't think you s_____ break up with her.

8 You look w_____.

6 ★★ **Complete the dialogue with the phrases from the box.**

- why don't you • I'm a bit worried about
- Maybe you should • What's up?
- I don't think you should
- ~~You look a bit miserable~~
- I don't know what to do

A: Hello, Seth. [1]_You look a bit miserable_.

[2]_____

B: [3]_____ my relationship with Rachael. We had an argument yesterday and she broke up with me.

[4]_____ about it.

A: I see. Well, [5]_____ phone her and apologise?

B: I tried that but she refused to talk to me.

A: [6]_____ send her some flowers first.

B: I haven't got any money for flowers. I think I'll go round to her house and bang on her front door until she agrees to talk to me.

A: [7]_____ do that. Her parents won't be very happy and she'll be even angrier with you. I'll lend you some money for flowers.

Grammar summary

Present perfect simple and past simple

Present perfect simple
I**'ve already eaten** dinner.
She**'s never been** late before.
Have you **asked** her out **yet**?
Past simple
I **ate** dinner **half an hour ago**.
She **wasn't** late **yesterday**.
Did you **ask** her out **last weekend**?

Note

Use

- We use the present perfect simple when the time period is unfinished or with certain time adverbials such as *just, yet* or *already*, which show a connection with the present.
  Have you ever been to America? (in your life)
  I've never been in love. (in my life)

- We use the past simple when the time period is finished.
  I went to the cinema yesterday.
  What did you do last weekend?

Common problems

- We can use some time expressions with both the present perfect simple and the past simple.
  Have you seen Ben this morning? (It is still morning.)
  Did you see Ben this morning? (It is now later in the day.)

Common mistakes

~~Did you ever fall in love?~~ ✗
Have you ever fallen in love? ✓

2c People who you can trust.

Vocabulary: Family

1 ⭐ **Look at the family tree and answer the questions.**

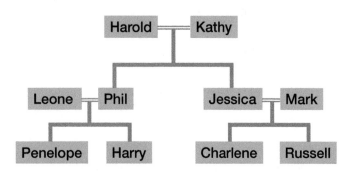

1 Who is Phil's wife?   _Leone_
2 Who is Harry's aunt?   _____
3 Who are Penelope's grandparents? _____
4 Who are Harry's cousins?   _____
5 Who is Kathy's son?   _____
6 Who is Russell's uncle?   _____
7 Who is Mark's daughter?   _____
8 Who is Phil's niece?   _____
9 Who is Jessica's brother?   _____
10 Who is Jessica's nephew?   _____

2 ⭐⭐ **Complete the sentences with the words from the box. There are three extra words.**

> • ~~mother-in-law~~ • sister-in-law
> • stepmother • stepfather • stepsister
> • single • fiancé • fiancée • married

1 Your wife's mother is your _mother-in-law_.
2 A person who doesn't have a husband or wife
   is _____.
3 The woman who married your father when he
   divorced your mum is your _____.
4 The boy you are engaged to is your
   _____.
5 Your husband's sister is your _____.
6 The girl you are engaged to is your _____.

Grammar: Defining relative clauses with *who, which, that, whose, where*

3 ⭐ **Complete the sentences with the relative pronouns from the box.**

> • ~~who~~ (x 2) • which • where (x 2) • whose

1 I've got a cousin _who_ plays football for Arsenal
   Under 16s.
2 This is the restaurant _____ my
   boyfriend proposed to me.
3 My sister is married to a man _____
   parents live in a castle.
4 This is the school _____ I want to go to.
5 I know a shop _____ you can work this
   summer.
6 The couple _____ were getting married
   didn't look very happy.

4 ⭐⭐ **Choose the option which is NOT possible.**

1 My girlfriend is someone …
   a) I love very much.   b) me very much.
   c) my parents get on with very well.
2 This is the church where …
   a) my parents got married in.
   b) a lot of local people get married.
   c) they filmed *Four Weddings and a Funeral*.
3 I want to meet someone whose …
   a) got a lot of money.   b) parents are rich.
   c) ideas about life are the same as mine.
4 The wedding …
   a) I remember best was my cousin's.
   b) we read about cost £10,000.
   c) took place here last week was between a
     prince and an actress.
5 I've met someone that …
   a) I love very much.   b) I care about him a lot.
   c) is never late.

5 ★★ **Complete the sentences with *who*, *which*, *where* or *whose*. Put the pronoun in brackets if it can be omitted.**

1 She's a girl *who* makes me smile every time I see her.

2 She's a girl *(who)* I can tell my secrets to.

3 That was a day _____ I will never forget.

4 That was the day _____ changed my life.

5 She's the girl _____ brother is a famous singer.

6 We went to a café _____ I never want to go back to again!

7 We went to a café _____ a sandwich cost £8!

6 ★★★ **Join the sentences with relative pronouns. Make any other changes necessary.**

1 She's a woman. Her husband was a famous footballer.

She's a woman whose husband was a famous footballer.

2 She's a woman. She was in a pop group.

_____

3 It's an art gallery. You can see the Mona Lisa there.

_____
_____

4 It's an art gallery. Lots of people visit it each year.

_____

5 He's an actor. He's won the Best Actor Oscar three times.

_____
_____

6 He's an actor. His father was a famous poet.

_____

7 It's a place. It's a district of Los Angeles.

_____
_____

8 It's a place. Lots of films are made there.

_____

Grammar summary

Defining relative clauses with *who, which, that, whose, where*
People (*who/that*)
I know a boy **who** was on television.
These are the people (**who/that**) I told you about.
Things (*which/that*)
My girlfriend said some things **which/that** annoyed me.
This is the shop (**which/that**) I buy most of my clothes from.
Possessions (*whose*)
Mr Clarke is the teacher **whose** tests are the most difficult.
Places (*where*)
This is the town **where** I grew up.

Note

Use

- We use defining relative clauses to give essential information about the person, place or thing we are talking about.
  That's the book which I was telling you about.

- In conversation and informal language, we often replace *who* or *which* with *that*.
  Is this the shop that refused to give you your money back?
  She's the girl that smiled at me.

Form

- We can omit *who, which* or *that* when they refer to the object of the sentence.
  That's the CD (which/that) I want to buy.
  She's the girl (who/that) I love.

- We can't miss out *where* or *whose*.

Common mistakes

~~This is the classroom where have exams in.~~ ✗
This is the classroom where we have exams. ✓
This is the classroom (which/that) we have exams in. ✓
~~This is the boy which I met at the disco.~~ ✗
This is the boy (who/that) I met at the disco. ✓

2 Language round-up

1 Complete the text with one word in each space.

> Hi Marcin,
>
> Thanks for your email. This is a photo of my family. My mum and dad ¹*got* divorced three years ²_____. She's going to ³_____ married to the man in the photo next year so I'll have a ⁴_____. He's got a son, Simon, so I'll have a ⁵_____, too. The other woman is my mum's sister, my ⁶_____. She hasn't got any children so I haven't got any ⁷_____.
> I hope I get ⁸_____ well with Simon. At least there will be someone else to help with the jobs in the house. I ⁹_____ the cooking every day. Of course, I ¹⁰_____ my bed in the morning and I ¹¹_____ my room every Saturday. After that, I'm free to go out. I usually go out with my friend Samantha but last week, she ¹²_____ in love with a boy at a party. He asked her ¹³_____ on Saturday but they may break ¹⁴_____ before then. Samantha doesn't stay with boys for very long! She always ¹⁵_____ an argument about something!
> Write soon.
>
> Lucy

.../14

2 Choose the correct options.

1 I've been to Italy twice but I've ___ seen Rome.
   a) ever   b) yet   c) never

2 Have you emptied the dishwasher ___?
   a) already   b) ever   c) yet

3 Did you enjoy the film ___?
   a) yesterday   b) already   c) yet

4 Have you seen Joe ___?
   a) yesterday   b) recently   c) last night

5 How much work have you done ___?
   a) so far   b) on Saturday   c) at the weekend

6 Where ___ you go yesterday?
   a) were   b) did   c) have

7 When ___ this photo?
   a) do you take   b) have you taken
   c) did you take

.../6

3 Complete the dialogue with the words from the box.

> • whose • went • yet • who • just
> • which • ~~Did~~ • has • out • ago • Have

Meg: ¹*Did* you see Jake last night? ²_____ you made up with him ³_____?

Jo: Yes, and we promised not to fall ⁴_____ again. There's a concert ⁵_____ his brother's band are going to play in on Saturday.

Meg: Saturday? We arranged to go to the cinema a long time ⁶_____.

Jo: I know but there will be someone at the concert ⁷_____ I think you'll want to meet. Tom Stephens. The boy ⁸_____ family moved to France when we were in Year 9. You were heartbroken! He's ⁹_____ come back. You ¹⁰_____ out with him, didn't you?

Meg: No, but I wanted to. OK, I'll be there. I wonder if he ¹¹_____ changed much.

.../10

4 Cross out the two incorrect words in each sentence and write the correct ones.

1 My cousin ~~is~~ just ~~gone~~ engaged. *has, got*

2 I get up very well with my cousin and I'm very close with her mum. _____

3 My parents haven't met Neil already, but they have saw his photo. _____

4 I fell on love with a boy what I met at a party. _____

5 You've never made the washing-up and you've never done your bed. _____

6 I find it easy to get friends with people I meet, but I often do arguments with my brother. _____

.../10

🎧 LISTEN AND CHECK YOUR SCORE	
Total	.../40

2 Skills practice

SKILLS FOCUS: READING, LISTENING AND WRITING

Read

1 Read the text and choose the best title.

A Max's big argument

B Max's mum makes a decision

C Max wants more freedom

Max was tired. He was always tired. His school books were open, but he couldn't concentrate. At that moment, his father walked into the room.

'Have you finished, your homework yet?' he said.

Max shouted, 'No, I haven't and I won't finish it if you keep coming in.'

His father gently said: 'You've done enough. Go to bed.'

This time, Max didn't argue and, he was soon asleep.

Downstairs, his mum was worried. 'He's so tired. He'll be ill,' she said.

The next day, Max apologised to his dad. 'I just don't know what to do. I've got lots of homework, Sylvia always wants to go out and I have to go to football practice, too.'

'You have to decide what's most important,' said his father.

Max knew he was right. He knew he was lucky that his parents didn't tell him what to do. 'But you can't go out with Sylvia from Sunday to Thursday,' said his mother, suddenly. His father looked at her in surprise. Max was shocked. 'But mum,' he said 'that's not fair.' But he was happy that his mum had decided for him!

2 Read the text again and answer true (T) or false (F).

1 At the start of the story, Max is working hard. _T_

2 Max's father tells Max what to do. ___

3 Max's parents are both worried about his health. ___

4 Max's problem is that he hasn't got enough time to do everything. ___

5 The person who makes Max's life easier in the end is his dad. ___

Listen

3 🎧 Listen to the conversation and decide who the two people are.

a) A boyfriend and girlfriend who have broken up.

b) A boyfriend and girlfriend.

c) A boy and a girl who are friends.

4 🎧 Listen again and answer the questions.

1 When is Shelly's party?

Wednesday

2 Who did Kevin Gates go out with in the past?

_____.

3 How did Kevin feel when they broke up?

_____.

4 What does Liz want Max to do?

_____.

5 When is Max going to talk to Sylvia?

_____.

Write

5 Complete the invitation with the words and phrases from the box.

- What about going • See you tomorrow
- It will be • are coming • Hi • tell me
- I'm not having • I'll ask • Do you want

¹_Hi_ Steve,

It's my birthday on Thursday. I hate having a birthday on a school day! ²_____ a normal day with an early start and homework! Friday will be a bit more exciting. My aunt and uncle and my two cousins ³_____ to our house for a small family party.

⁴_____ a party for friends this year, but I'd like to do something. ⁵_____ to go to the cinema with me on Saturday? There's a good action film on at four o'clock in the afternoon.

⁶_____ into town early and having a pizza or something for lunch first? I think ⁷_____ Heather and Sally, too.

Think about it and ⁸_____ at school tomorrow.

⁹_____.

Max.

3a Too big to see it all on foot.

Grammar: *too* + adjective/adverb +
to; *(not)* + adjective/adverb + *enough to*

1 ⭐ **Complete the sentences with one word in each space.**

1 I wrote carefully, but I didn't write carefully *enough*.

2 I swam well, but I didn't swim well enough _____ win.

3 I worked hard, but I didn't work _____ enough to pass my exam.

4 I wrote my test _____ quickly and made lots of mistakes.

5 I spoke quietly, but I didn't speak quietly _____ and my teacher heard me.

2 ⭐⭐ **Use the prompts to write sentences.**

Where do you want to go for your winter holiday?

1 Moscow?

It/cold *It's too cold.*

2 Jamaica?

a) It/far _____.

b) I/not rich _____.

3 Skiing?

a) I/scared _____.

b) It/dangerous _____.

4 Rome?

a) It/rainy _____.

b) My Italian/not good

_____.

5 London

a) It/big _____.

b) The food/not tasty

_____.

3 ⭐⭐⭐ **Complete the second sentence so that it has the same meaning as the first. Use the word in capitals.**

1 I'm too young to go on holiday with my friends. ENOUGH

I'm *not old enough to go on holiday with my friends*.

2 My PC is too slow for this game. FAST

My PC _____.

3 I was too slow to win the race. RAN

I _____.

4 I'm not tall enough to play for the school basketball team. SHORT

I'm _____.

5 I'm not good enough at French to understand this book. SPEAK

I don't _____.

6 We can't go out for a meal because all the restaurants are shut. LATE

It's _____.

Vocabulary: Adjectives and nouns of measurement

4 ⭐ **Complete the text with one word in each space.**

The London Eye is great. It's quite [1]e*xpensive*. Tickets cost about £20 each for adults, but it's worth it. The Eye is 135 metres [2]h_____ so you get a great view from the top. There are thirty-two glass rooms that you stand in for your journey. They are very [3]b_____. Twenty-five people can go in each one and there is still lots of room to move around. The Eye isn't very [4]f_____. It's slow enough for people to get on and off easily.

It isn't very [5]o_____, but I can't imagine London without it. Big Ben isn't very [6]f_____ from The Eye and it's a nice walk. You just cross the River Thames, which is about 200 metres [7]w_____, on Westminster Bridge, which is about 250 metres [8]l_____.

Vocabulary: Transport

5 ⭐ **Match the definitions (1–9) to the words (a–i).**

1 You cycle on this.   e

2 It's like a small motorbike.   —

3 You fly in this.   —

4 You can phone for one to take you
  where you want to go.   —

5 It's like a train but below the city.   —

6 It's like a big car (or a small lorry).   —

7 You can catch this at a railway station.   —

8 It travels on water.   —

9 You drive it.   —

a) underground   f) van

b) train   g) car

c) moped   h) helicopter

d) boat   i) taxi

e) bike

6 ⭐⭐ **Look at the pictures and complete the puzzle.**

1	S	C	O	O	T	E	R

2 R
3 A
4 N
5 S
6 P
7 O
8 R
9 T

Grammar summary

too + adjective/adverb + *to*

You're **too young to** buy fireworks.

She types **too slowly to** be a secretary.

(not) + adjective/adverb + *enough to*

You're **clever enough to** get into university.

She **runs fast** enough to be a sports star.

He is**n't strong enough to** lift his bags.

He does**n't sing well enough** to win the competition.

Note

Use

- We use *too* + adjective/adverb + *to* and *(not)* + adjective/adverb + *enough* + *to* to say that something is not possible.
  He's too young to play with us. (It's impossible for him to play with us because of his age.)
  She speaks too quietly to be an actress. (It's impossible for her to be an actress because of the quietness of her voice.)

- We use adjective/adverb + *enough* + *to* to say something is possible.
  She's good enough to win this competition. (It is possible for her to win this competition.)

- We don't use *too* or *enough* with adjectives which don't have comparative or superlative forms, e.g. *impossible, dead, English* – things can't be more or less impossible, dead or English.

Common mistakes

~~He is enough old to understand the rules.~~ ✗
He is old enough to understand the rules. ✓
~~He's too unfit for being a footballer.~~ ✗
He's too unfit to be a footballer. ✓

3b You can't miss it.

Vocabulary: Places in town

1 ⭐ **Match the beginnings (1–10) to the endings (a–g) to make places in town. Some beginnings match the same ending.**

1 swimming	a) centre
2 petrol	b) gallery
3 police	c) pool
4 sports	d) station
5 town	e) shop
6 tourist information	f) office
7 music	g) hall
8 art	
9 post	
10 shopping	

2 ⭐⭐ **Complete the places.**

1 My mum works here. She sells coffee and cakes.   c<u>afé</u>

2 Mr Smith works here. People go to him to ask for money or give him their money.
   b_____

3 Three hundred people work here. They make cars.   f_____

4 Miss Jenkins, the nurse, and Miss Taylor, the doctor, work here.   h_____

5 We get our daily newspaper from here.
   n_____

6 My friend worked here with ten other people. They all had a desk and a computer. My friend hated it.   o_____

7 You can book your holiday on the internet or you can go here.   t_____ a_____

8 When I want a book to read, I go here.
   l_____

9 You can get a holiday job as a waiter here.
   r_____

10 It's a great place to buy food. It's cheaper than smaller shops.   s_____

3 ⭐⭐ **Complete the description with one letter in each space.**

Our town is very beautiful. In the centre of the town is a lovely [1]s<u>quare</u> with cafés and beautiful old buildings. There's an interesting [2]_ _ s _ u _ where you can find out about the town's history. Not far from the centre, there is a big [3]_ _ r _ with trees and grass. It's a great place to walk on a sunny day and there's a small [4]_ o _ with animals like wolves and deer in it. There aren't any elephants or lions, though. There's a [5]_ h _ _ t _ _ where you can see great plays. There are two [6]_ _ t _ _ s where you can stay the night. One is big and expensive, but the smaller one is nicer. Oh, and in Station Road, just past the [7]_ h _ _ m _ c _, is my [8]_ c _ _ _ l.

Phrases

4 ⭐⭐ **Choose the correct options.**

Mike: Excuse me.

Tracey: Yes?

Mike: I'm a bit [1]**far** / (**lost**) / **wrong**. I'm trying to get to the café.

Tracey: The café?

Mike: Oh, I [2]**think** / **mean** / **suppose** there are lots of cafés.

Tracey: Yes, there are. Tell me about the one you want.

Mike: Eh?

Tracey: I [3]**guess** / **suppose** / **mean** what it looks like, what kind of food it sells.

Mike: Oh. It's French. It's got very good cakes.

Tracey: Oh, I know. 'Le Soleil'. Come with me.

Mike: Thanks … is it far … through the park? Wow, it's a long way … Ah, at last, the town centre. What [4]**more** / **now** / **for**?

Tracey: We just cross the road and it's over there. Look.

Mike: Oh great. Thanks. Can I buy you a cake?

Tracey: Mmm, I'd love one.

Use your English: Ask for and give directions

5 ⭐ **Match the pictures to the directions from the box.**

> • Go straight on.   • ~~Turn right~~.
> • Cross the road.   • Take the first on the right.
> • Turn left.   • The bank is next to the station.
> • Go past the bank.   • Take the second on the left.
> • The bank is opposite the station.
> • Go right out of the station.

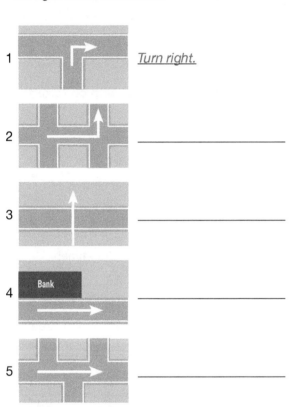

1   _Turn right._

2   _____

3   _____

4   _____

5   _____

6   _____

7   _____

8   _____

9   _____

10 _____

6 ⭐⭐ **Complete the dialogues with one word in each space.**

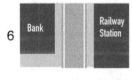

1   **A:** Excuse me. How can I get to the theatre?

 B: Go ¹_right_ out of the station and ²_____ the first turning on your ³_____. Go ⁴_____ the pharmacy and turn ⁵_____. The theatre is ⁶_____ the supermarket.

2   **A:** How can I get to the museum from the hospital?

 B: Go left ⁷_____ of the hospital and turn ⁸_____ at the corner. Take the ⁹_____ turning on your left and go straight on. At the corner, turn right and the museum is on the left ¹⁰_____ to the library.

7 ⭐⭐⭐ **Complete the dialogues with one word in each space.**

1   **A:** ¹_Excuse_ me. Can you tell me the ²_____ to the post office, please?

 B: Yes, of course. Go ³_____ on along this road for about 200 metres. Go ⁴_____ the supermarket and then ⁵_____ the road at the traffic lights. You'll see the post office ⁶_____ your right.

2   **A:** Sorry to ⁷_____ you, but ⁸_____ do I get to the sports centre?

 B: Go left ⁹_____ of here. ¹⁰_____ the third turning on your left. That's Chapel Street. The sports centre is next ¹¹_____ an Italian restaurant.

 A: Thank you.

 B: You're ¹²_____.

3c We throw away too many things.

Vocabulary: Countable and uncountable nouns

1 ⭐ **Choose the option which is NOT possible.**

1 There are a lot of ___.
   a) rubbish   b) holes   c) problems

2 There is some ___ in the kitchen.
   a) food   b) things   c) luggage

3 I've got a big ___.
   a) family   b) children   c) problem

4 We need more ___.
   a) informations   b) news   c) schools

5 We've got a problem with ___.
   a) pollution   b) traffic   c) factory

6 There aren't many ___.
   a) money   b) gardens   c) streets

2 ⭐⭐ **Tick (✓) the sentences which are correct. Put a cross (✗) after the sentences which are incorrect.**

1 I haven't got a food. ✗
2 There isn't any food. ✓
3 How many children are there?
4 My sister's got a child.
5 How can you carry all these luggages?
6 Is that luggage heavy?
7 There's a lot of rubbish in the street.
8 There's a rubbish in the hall.
9 There are lots of plastic.
10 Have you got a plastic?
11 I haven't got any money.
12 How many money have you got?
13 The news today was very interesting.
14 I heard an interesting news this morning.

Grammar: too many, too much, not enough

3 ⭐ **Complete the sentences with too much, too many, aren't enough or isn't enough.**

1 There's _too much_ rubbish.
2 There _____ information.
3 There are _____ holes in the roads.
4 There _____ shops in this town.
5 There _____ good music on the radio.
6 There _____ things to do in the evenings.
7 There are _____ noisy children in this class.
8 There is _____ pollution from this factory.

4 ⭐⭐ **Complete the dialogues with one word or contraction in each space.**

A A: Why don't you like your school?
   B: I don't like it because we get
      ¹_too_ _much_ homework and we have
      ² _____ _____ exams. There
      ³ _____ _____ holidays and there
      ⁴ _____ _____ free time!

B A: Why don't you play outside?
   B: There ⁵_____ _____ parks
      and green spaces. I can't play in the street
      because there's ⁶_____ _____
      traffic and there's ⁷_____ _____
      pollution. I can't play in the garden because
      there ⁸_____ _____ room – Mum
      and Dad have got ⁹_____ _____
      flowers!

C A: Why don't you like holidays?
   B: We always take ¹⁰_____ _____
      luggage. It's really heavy. We don't
      have ¹¹_____ money for taxis.
      Planes are always late and there
      ¹²_____ _____ information
      about the flights so you wait in the airport
      for hours. At the hotel, there are always
      ¹³_____ _____ old people and
      there ¹⁴_____ never _____ children
      of my age.

Grammar: Pronouns *some-, any-, no-, every- + thing, where, one, body*

5 ⭐ **Complete the sentences with the pronouns from the box.**

- nobody • nowhere • anywhere
- somewhere • ~~anything~~ • anyone
- nothing • Everyone

1 Have you got *anything* to wear to the party?

2 We've got _____ to eat. Why didn't you go shopping?

3 There's _____ to go in the evening. It's a really boring town.

4 It was great! _____ I met was really nice.

5 What a terrible party. There's _____ here.

6 I don't want to go _____ this weekend.

7 Do you know _____ who is interested in the environment?

8 Let's go _____ different this summer.

6 ⭐⭐ **Complete the dialogues with the correct pronouns.**

1 **A:** I want to go *somewhere* warm this summer. I want to meet _____ rich and handsome. I want to do _____ exciting.

B: So you don't want to go camping?

2 **A:** Are you OK?

B: No. I had a terrible day. _____ went wrong. I was late and the exam was difficult. I don't want to do _____ this evening. I don't want to talk to _____ and I don't want to go _____.

A: But _____'s going to Michelle's party.

B: No, they aren't. I'm not going.

3 **A:** You look upset. What's wrong?

B: I don't want to talk about it. _____ can help me. There's _____ I can do. There's _____ I can go to escape.

A: This sounds terrible.

B: It is. My mum wants me to tidy my room.

Grammar summary

too many, too much, not enough

Our teachers give us **too many** tests.
There is **too much** traffic.
There **wasn't enough** information.
I think there **is enough** food now.

Note

Use

- We use *too many* with plural, countable nouns.
  There are too many people here.
- We use *too much* with uncountable nouns.
  We waste too much electricity.
- We use *(not) enough* with countable and uncountable nouns.
  There aren't enough people.
  There isn't enough money.

Pronouns *some-, any-, no-, every- + thing, where, one, body*

There's **someone/somebody** in the kitchen.
Have you got **anything** to eat?
There's **nowhere** to swim in this town.
I take my camera **everywhere** I go.

Note

Use

- We use pronouns with *some* when the identity of the person, thing or place is unknown.
  Someone picked up my bag by mistake.
- We use pronouns with *any* in questions and negative sentences.
  I didn't see anything.
- We use pronouns with *no* in positive sentences. They have the same meaning as *any* in negative sentences.
  I didn't see anything. = I saw nothing.
- We use pronouns with *every* in positive sentences to mean all the people, all the things, all the places.
  Everyone in my class forgot their homework. = All the people in my class forgot.

Common mistakes

- We don't use *no one, nobody, nothing* or *nowhere* in negative sentences.
  ~~I haven't seen no one today.~~ ✗
  I haven't seen anyone today. ✓

3 Language round-up

1 Complete the text with the words from the box.

- art galleries • traffic • ~~train~~ • boat
- underground • parks • expensive
- theatre • restaurant • taxis • far

Last month my parents and I went to London. We got there by [1]_train_. At the station, lots of [2]_____ were waiting so we took one to our hotel. The hotel was quite [3]_____ from the centre so we travelled everywhere by [4]_____. There was a station near our hotel. We had a great time. We saw a play by Shakespeare at a [5]_____ and we visited lots of interesting museums and [6]_____. London is an [7]_____ city, but a lot of museums are free to visit. We ate in a great [8]_____.

On the second day, we went along the River Thames by [9]_____. The only problem with London is the [10]_____. The roads are always busy, but there are lots of [11]_____ with trees, flowers and grass where you can relax.

…/10

2 Choose the correct options.

I wanted to buy a stamp but [1]**somebody** / **nobody** knew the way to the post office. One man told me to [2]**turn** / **take** the first turning on the left. It was the wrong way. Then [3]**someone** / **anyone** told me to walk [4]**along** / **past** the market, but I didn't see a market [5]**nowhere** / **anywhere**. There were some tourist information [6]**agents** / **centres**, but [7]**anything** / **nothing** was open. In the end, I went back to my hotel. I was [8]**too** / **enough** tired to do anything else that day. I didn't have [9]**enough** / **too many** money to eat in the hotel restaurant so I went to a [10]**supermarket** / **pharmacy** and bought a sandwich. Then I found that they sold stamps, too. All that walking and there were stamps for sale right next [11]**by** / **to** the hotel!

…/10

3 Cross out the incorrect word in each sentence and write the correct one.

1 ~~Where~~ do I get to the bus station?   _How_
2 There are too much cars here.   _____
3 Buses are too slowly.   _____
4 Are this your luggage, sir?   _____
5 We haven't had nothing to eat yet.   _____
6 The deep of the river here is ten metres.   _____
7 The man in the travel agent's gave me some useful informations.   _____
8 There's anything good on TV. Let's watch a DVD.   _____
9 There is not enough bookshops in my town.   _____
10 How width is this bridge?   _____
11 I hated walking round Paris. There was too many traffic.   _____

…/10

4 Complete the text with one word in each space.

Hi Rose,

I'm glad you can come to my party. The best way to [1]_get_ to my house is by bus. The house isn't [2]_____ from the bus station. Go out of the bus station and [3]_____ right. Walk past the post [4]_____ and then [5]_____ the first turning [6]_____ the left. My house is next [7]_____Tom's Café, opposite the park. I've invited seven people. I wanted to ask the whole class, but my mum said that was too [8]_____ people and that our house isn't big [9]_____ to have a big party. Maybe she's right. With a small party, there won't be too [10]_____ rubbish to clear up afterwards!
I think that's enough information for you. Phone me if you need to know [11]_____ else.
See you on Saturday.

Love, Donna

…/10

LISTEN AND CHECK YOUR SCORE

Total	…/40

3 Skills practice

SKILLS FOCUS: READING AND **WRITING**

Read

1 Read the text and complete the places (1–3) with one word in each space.

1 The _____ _____

2 The _____ Museum

3 The _____ _____ Mall

> **Washington DC**, the capital of the USA, is probably best known for The White House, where the President lives. However, there is much more to see.

1

The Washington Monument has a height of 170 metres. It is over 100 years old and took over thirty years to build. The Monument is in The National Mall, very close to The White House.

2

There are nineteen museums and a zoo in the Smithsonian Museum. These include the Natural History Museum and the Museum of Air and Space. Most of the museums and the zoo are free and they are open 364 days of the year.

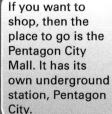

3

If you want to shop, then the place to go is the Pentagon City Mall. It has its own underground station, Pentagon City.

2 Read the text again and choose the correct options.

1 The Washington Monument is **100** / **170** metres high.

2 The Washington Monument is over **100** / **30** years old.

3 The **Washington Monument** / **White House** is in the National Mall.

4 The Smithsonian is **nineteen** / **one of nineteen** museums in Washington.

5 The zoo is **the only part** / **one part** of the Smithsonian which is free.

6 Pentagon City is the name of **a hotel** / **an underground station**.

Write

3 Look at the brochure and match the topic sentences (a–d) to the spaces (1–4).

a) Siracusa is a perfect city for walking.

b) The Piazza Duomo is the heart of the city.

c) There is no need for supermarkets in Siracusa.

d) When it's time to relax, the Italians know best.

Siracusa, Sicily's jewel

[1] *b* You could spend your whole holiday here. However, the small lanes and roads leading off in every direction also need to be explored.

[2] ___ The old city, on the island of Ortygia, is small enough to be explored on foot in a day or two. Many of the streets are almost traffic free.

[3] ___ Siracusa is full of cafés. The locals sit outside, watching the world go by. When you need a rest, why not do the same?

[4] ___ For fresh food, the outdoor market is the place to go. Every day, you can find fresh fruit, vegetables, cheese and, best of all, fish from the Mediterranean Sea.

4 Write a brochure about a place that you know. Use the topic sentences to start your paragraphs.

1 The town really comes to life in the evenings.

2 There are lots of places to go to relax.

3 Use the local transport to see the town.

4 You don't need money to enjoy yourself.

4a I haven't seen the sun for weeks.

4 TIME PASSES

Vocabulary: Collocations with *make* and *do*

1 ★ **Put the phrases from the box in the correct column.**

- an appointment • some exercise
- your best • a decision
- your homework • the shopping
- a noise • friends with someone
- the housework • a cake

Make	Do
a cake	_____
_____	_____
_____	_____
_____	_____
_____	_____

2 ★★ **Complete the sentences with the correct form of *make* or *do*.**

1 I've thought of a great way to *make* some money.

2 I've _____ you some sandwiches for your journey.

3 You're so lazy. It's midday and you haven't _____ anything yet.

4 We're _____ Physics at school this year.

5 You can have a party, but please don't _____ a mess.

6 I had a Maths test today and I _____ lots of mistakes.

7 You lay the table and I'll _____ dinner.

8 Tom is studying hard and it's _____ a difference to his marks.

Grammar: Present perfect simple with *for* and *since*

3 ★ **Complete the sentences with one word in each space.**

1  I've been here <u>*since*</u> two o'clock.
I've been here <u>*for*</u> two hours.
It's now <u>*four*</u> o'clock.

2  Mark has been in this class _____ five months.
Mark has been in this class _____ September.
It's now _____.

3  We've lived here _____ 2001.
We've lived here _____ 12 years.
It's now _____.

4  Tom has been asleep _____ nine o'clock last night.
Tom has been asleep _____ 13 hours.
It's now _____ o'clock in the morning.

5  Steve and Kathy have been together _____ two weeks.
Steve and Kathy have been together _____ 7th January.
It's now the twenty-_____ of January.

4 ⭐⭐ **Use the prompts to write sentences.**

1 I met Jackie three years ago.

   I've known Jackie for three years. (I/know/for)

2 I bought this book last week.

   _____ (I/have/for)

3 I started at this school in 2008.

   _____ (I/be/since)

4 The last time I saw this film was five years ago.

   _____ (I/not see/for)

5 The last time Tim was late for school was last year.

   _____ (Tim/not be/since)

6 Meg arrived here thirty seconds ago.

   _____ (Meg/be/for)

7 The last time my dad had a holiday was in 2010.

   _____ (My dad/not have/since)

5 ⭐⭐⭐ **Use the prompts to write questions and answers.**

1 A: How long/you know/Simon?

   B: I/know him/three years

   A: How long have you known Simon?

   B: I've known him for three years.

2 A: How long/your mum/be a teacher?

   B: She/be/a teacher/1993

   _____

   _____

3 A: How long/you like/Justin Bieber?

   B: I/like/him/last year

   _____

   _____

4 A: How long/you have/a dog?

   B: We/have/her/about two months

   _____

   _____

5 A: How long/this building/be here?

   B: It/be/here/2009

   _____

   _____

Grammar summary

Present perfect simple with *for* and *since*

Affirmative

I **have been** here **for** two hours/**since** three o'clock.

He **has lived** here **for** ten years/**since** 2003.

Negative

They **haven't seen** Paul **for** three days/**since** Tuesday.

She **hasn't watched** television **for** months/**since** before Christmas.

Questions

How long **have** you **had** that phone?

I**'ve had** it **for** two weeks/**since** my birthday.

Note

Use

- We use the Present perfect simple with *for* and *since* to talk about how long a situation that started in the past has existed.

  I have lived here for ten years. = I started living here ten years ago and I still live here now.

- We use *for* with a period of time to show how long a situation has existed.

  He's known me for a long time.

- We use *since* with a point in time to show when the situation or action started.

  She's been here since Friday.

- When we use a verb to give the point in time after *since*, we use the past simple.

  I've known him since we were young.

Common mistakes

~~We are here since 2010.~~ ✗

We've been here since 2010. ✓

~~We've known each other since three years.~~ ✗

We've known each other for three years. ✓

~~I've lived here since I have been five.~~ ✗

I've lived here since I was five. ✓

4b You've been talking for ages.

Phrases

1 ⭐ Complete the dialogues with the words from the box.

> • tell • in • ~~ages~~ • just • about • last • on

1 **A:** Hurry up in the bathroom. You've been in there for _ages_.

  B: I've finished.

  A: At _____!

2 **A:** I can get us tickets for the concert.

  B: How? There aren't any left.

  A: Let's _____ say that I know someone who can help us.

  B: Don't _____ me. Your dad got some from work.

3 **A:** I'm writing an article. It's _____ bullying. Do you want to help me?

  B: OK, yes. I'm _____. I hate bullying.

  A: Great. We're _____ it!

Vocabulary: Phrasal verbs with *look*

2 ⭐ Complete the sentences with one word in each space.

1 Sue and Tom are looking _at_ the elephant.

2 Paul is looking _____ a new word in his dictionary.

3 Sam is looking _____ to the holidays.

4 Rebecca is looking _____ her phone.

5 Sophie is looking _____ her little brother.

3 ⭐⭐ Complete the texts with the correct form of phrasal verbs with *look*.

Hi Sue,
I need to ask for your help. I agreed to ¹*look after* my neighbour's cat, but he's disappeared. I've been ² _____ it all day. Can you come and help me?
Thanks, **Becky** x

Hi Maria,
I'm really ³ _____ seeing you in Spain soon. I've been learning Spanish – I've been ⁴ _____ new words in the dictionary and ⁵ _____ photos of Granada. It's beautiful. I can't believe I'll be there in two weeks!
All the best, **Laura** x

Grammar: Present perfect continuous with *for* and *since*

4 ⭐ Complete the sentences with the correct form of the verbs in brackets and *for* or *since*.

1 Paul _has been watching_ (watch) television _since_ five o'clock.

2 I _____ (read) this book _____ three weeks.

3 You _____ (talk) on the telephone _____ ages.

4 Danny _____ (learn) Spanish _____ he was ten.

5 Lisa _____ (sing) she was a young girl.

6 It _____ (rain) hours.

7 They _____ (go) out together _____ last September.

5 ★★ Use the prompts to complete the dialogues.

1 A: Hi, Carol. What have you been doing this morning?

  B: _I've been reading_. (I/read)

  A: How long have you been reading for?

  B: _____ (I/read/two hours.)

2 A: Steven looks tired. How long has he been swimming for?

  B: _____ (He/swim/four o'clock)

  A: Really? _____ (So/he/swim/two hours.) He should come out now.

  B: _____ (I/tell/him to come out/half an hour.)

  A: I'll tell him. Steven! Out! Now!

6 ★★★ Use the prompts to complete the dialogues.

1 A: Hello. I haven't seen you for two years. _What have you been doing since I last saw you?_ (what/you do/I last see you)

  B: _____ (I cycle/around Europe)

  A: For two years?

  B: No, I got back last year.
_____ (I work/October)

2 A: _____ (you/wait long?)

  B: _____ (✓)
_____ (I wait/45 minutes)

  A: Sorry. _____ (I shop)

  B: Don't worry. _____ (I watch/that boy and girl/the last ten minutes) _____ (They argue/they arrived)

  A: Why?

  B: I don't know. _____ (I/not listen to their conversation!)

Grammar summary

Present perfect continuous with *for* and *since*

Affirmative
I've (have) been waiting for an hour.
You've (have) been working since two o'clock.
She's (has) been watching us for ten minutes.
He's (has) been playing tennis since ten to one.

Negative
We haven't been eating for three hours.
They haven't been crying since last night.
He hasn't been sleeping for ten hours.
She hasn't been swimming since midday.

Questions
How long have you been working?
I've been working for two hours/since ten o'clock.
What have you been doing all morning?

Note

Use

- We use the present perfect continuous to talk about activities which started in the past and which are still happening now or which have very recently stopped and have a present result.
  I've been working for two hours.
- We don't use stative verbs such as *like, want, understand* with the present perfect continuous.
  I've liked history since I was young. NOT *I've been liking history since I was young.*
- We can use the present perfect continuous to describe activities that aren't necessarily happening at this moment.
  She's been acting for ten years. (She may not be acting at the moment.)

Common mistakes

I've been knowing Simon since we were at school. ✗
I've known Simon since we were at school. ✓
I'm waiting here for half an hour. ✗
I've been waiting here for half an hour. ✓

4c She used to be a Goth.

Grammar: *used to*

1 ⭐ **Complete the sentences with the correct form of the words in brackets.**

1 (use/work)

My dad *used to work* in London, but now he works at home.

2 (use/be)

My mum _____ a teacher, but now she works in an office.

3 (not/use/like)

I _____ heavy metal, but now I love it.

4 (not/use/work)

My sister _____ very hard, but now she's the best student in her class.

5 (you/use/go)

_____ out with Melanie? Yes, but we broke up.

6 (she/use/have)

_____ red hair? No, it was blond.

7 (use/work)

I _____ in a restaurant on Saturdays, but now I haven't got time.

8 (your brother/use/go)

_____ skiing? Yes, but he broke his leg.

2 ⭐⭐ **Complete the text with the verbs from the box and the correct form of *used to*.**

- play (x 2) • wear • not wear • ~~ride~~
- cycle • go • make • dream

Me and my family ten years ago

I [1]*used to ride* my bike every day. I [2]_____ really fast! I loved my red T-shirt. I [3]_____ it all the time. My sister wore dresses all the time. She [4]_____ trousers. She didn't like them. She had a favourite doll. She [5]_____ with it every day. My sister and I [6]_____ together a lot. We [7]_____ a lot of noise, but we were happy. We didn't have a car. Our parents [8]_____ everywhere. I [9]_____ of having a car, but now I cycle everywhere, too.

3 ⭐⭐⭐ **Use the prompts to write questions and answers with *used to*.**

1 A: What sports/you/use/play/when you were younger?

A: *What sports did you use to play when you were younger?*

B: I/use/have/tennis lessons but I/not/use/like them

_____

2 A: What music/you/use/like/when you were ten?

_____

B: I/use/like/pop music. I not use/listen to/rock at all.

_____

3 A: Where/you and your family/use/go/on holiday when you were younger?

_____

B: We/use/go/to Cornwall. We/not use/go abroad.

_____

4 A: your/dad/use/have/long hair?

_____

B: No/not but my mum/use/have/pink hair!

_____

Grammar: Echo questions

4 ⭐ **Complete the echo questions with the correct verb.**

1 I've been waiting for ages.　　*Have* you?

2 I haven't finished yet.　　_____ you?

3 We used to live here.　　_____ you?

4 Lucy doesn't want to come to the disco.　　_____ she?

5 Gavin's late again.　　_____ he?

6 They're here already.　　_____ they?

7 I didn't use to like cheese.　　_____ you?

8 My dad isn't going to help us.　　_____ he?

5 ★★ **Complete the dialogues with the correct echo questions.**

1 **A:** I've got the computer game you told me about.

   B: *Have you*? Great!

   A: But it doesn't work.

   B: _____? Why not?

   A: I don't know.

2 **A:** My dad used to be a punk rocker.

   B: _____?

   A: Yes, and my mum was a Goth.

   B: _____? I thought she was a punk.

   A: _____? What made you think that?

3 **A:** I used to love Britney Spears.

   B: _____? I never liked her.

   A: _____? Not even when she sang *Toxic*?

   B: What?

   A: *Toxic*. It's really famous.

   B: _____? I've never heard of it.

Use your English: Show interest

6 ★★ **Choose the option which is NOT possible.**

1 **A:** I had a really bad day at school today.

   B: a) Did you?   b) Have you?   c) Really?

2 **A:** We're in the school's basketball final!

   B: a) How exciting!   b) Are you?   c) Why not?

3 **A:** Paul doesn't want to come to my party.

   B: a) Isn't he?   b) Really?   c) Why not?

4 **A:** I need a summer job.

   B: a) Why?   b) How awful!   c) Do you?

5 **A:** This used to be a park.

   B: a) Is it?   b) Really?   c) Did it?

6 **A:** My girlfriend broke up with me.

   B: a) Why?   b) Really?   c) Did you?

   A: She's met someone else.

   B: a) How awful!   b) Has she?
   c) How amazing!

Grammar summary

used to

used to	
Affirmative	
I **used to** live in France.	
She **used to** go swimming every day.	
Negative	
He didn't **use to** listen to classical music.	
Questions	
Did she **use to** watch television all day?	
Short answers	
Yes, I **did**. No, she **didn't**.	
Wh- questions	
Where **did** they **use to** live?	

Note

Use
- We use *used to* for past habits and states which are no longer true.
- We can't use *used to* to talk about things which only happened once in the past.

Form
- The form is the same for all persons:
- In negatives, we use *didn't* + *use* + *to* + the infinitive.
- In questions, we use *did* + subject + *use* + *to* + the infinitive.

Common mistakes

~~I didn't used to wear glasses.~~ ✗
I didn't use to wear glasses. ✓

Echo questions

Echo questions	
Affirmative	
A: I'm sixteen. B: **Are you?**	
A: He likes you. B: **Does he?**	
A: We've been here before. B: **Have you?**	
Negative	
A: You aren't in the final. B: **Aren't I?**	
A: She didn't go to school yesterday. B: **Didn't she?**	
A: They can't speak French. B: **Can't they?**	

Note

Use
- We use echo questions to show we are listening and are interested. The listener isn't asking a real question.

Form
- We make echo questions by using the correct auxiliary verb + the subject pronoun.
- The negative form of *I am* is *Aren't I.*

1 Match the questions (1–7) to the answers (a–g).

1 Has she been playing tennis long?   _d_

2 Why can't you go out tonight?   ___

3 Did you use to play with dolls?   ___

4 What are you looking for?   ___

5 What is she making?   ___

6 How long have you been here?   ___

7 What are they doing?   ___

a) My camera.   e) The ironing.

b) A cake.   f) I'm looking after my sister.

c) No, I didn't.   g) Since three o'clock.

d) Yes, she has.

.../6

2 Complete the dialogue with one word in each space.

Natalie: Hi, Sally. What's up?

Sally: I can't go to your party.

Natalie: Why ¹_not_?

Sally: Mum wants me to look ²_____ my brother.

Natalie: Oh no. We've ³_____ planning this party ⁴_____ ages.

Sally: I know. I've been really looking ⁵_____ to it.

Natalie: Can't you talk to your mum about it?

Sally: I've been talking to her ⁶_____ she told me, but I can't ⁷_____ anything about it. She says she's ⁸_____ her decision and that's it.

Natalie: Wait a minute, I've got an idea.

Sally: ⁹_____ you?

Natalie: Yes. How old is your brother?

Sally: He's twelve.

Natalie: ¹⁰_____ he? Well, you could bring him to the party.

Sally: No way.

Natalie: ¹¹_____ not? I ¹²_____ to take my little sister to parties.

Sally: ¹³_____ you?

Natalie: Yes. She loved them. Ask your mum.

.../12

3 Complete the second sentence so that it has the same meaning as the first. Use the word in capitals.

1 I've arranged a visit to get my hair cut. APPOINTMENT

I've _made an appointment_ for a haircut.

2 I never liked shopping when I was young. USE

I _____ shopping when I was young.

3 Can you take care of my dog next week? LOOK

Can you _____ when I'm on holiday?

4 I got this scarf on my birthday. HAD

I've _____ my birthday.

5 We started going out three weeks ago. BEEN

We _____ three weeks.

6 Was your sister noisy when she was a baby? BE

Did your sister _____ when she was a baby?

7 We always went for a walk in the evenings when we were in Spain. GO

We always _____ for a walk in the evenings when we were in Spain.

.../12

4 Use the prompts to write questions.

1 How long/you/wear/glasses?

How long have you been wearing glasses?

2 your sister/use/go out/on school nights?

_____

3 you/play/football/a long time?

_____

4 How long/your parents/have that car?

_____

5 How/you/use/get to primary school?

_____

6 How long/you/have/a headache?

_____

.../10

🎧 **LISTEN AND CHECK YOUR SCORE**

Total	.../40

4 Skills practice

SKILLS FOCUS: READING, LISTENING AND WRITING

Read

1 Read the text and answer true (T) or false (F).

1 The writer's grandfather has always lived in the same town. _T_

2 The air was cleaner in the past. ___

3 There aren't any factories open in the town now. ___

4 The writer's grandfather went out two evenings a week. ___

5 He didn't use to go to the cinema because of the smoke. ___

My grandfather is 73 and he's lived in this town since he was born. He's seen a lot of changes. One good thing is that the town is much cleaner now. When my grandfather was growing up, there wasn't much traffic but there were a lot of factories. On some days, the air used to be so dirty that people stayed indoors and there didn't use to be any fish in the river. Now, the factories have all gone. There is a lot of traffic and there's still some pollution, but there are more parks and the river has been clean since the 1980s.

My grandfather had a good childhood. He was a teenager when rock and roll was popular. He used to go dancing every Friday and Saturday. He didn't have much money, but everything was cheap. His family didn't have a television, but there was a cinema in the town centre. People used to smoke in the cinema! It was as polluted as the air outside, but my grandfather's parents used to take him every week when he was a boy and they used to sit in the smoky air. I can't believe he's still so healthy!

Listen

2 🎧 Listen to the conversation and answer the questions.

Who …

1 has been studying the wrong subject? _Peter_

2 is going out this evening? _____

3 doesn't like black and white films? _____

4 works better in the evening than in the morning? _____

3 🎧 Listen again and complete the sentences.

1 The two people have got a _History_ exam tomorrow.

2 The Geography exam is next _____.

3 Peter goes to film club every _____.

4 Film Noir films are usually _____.

5 Peter is going to study for the exam in the _____.

6 Peter and his girlfriend had an argument because he fell asleep in the _____.

Write

4 Use the notes to complete the report about a special building.

- Name: The Shard
- Opened: 1st February 2013
- Height: 306 metres
- Floors: 72
- Designer: Renzo Piano
- Where it is: Southwark
- How to get to it: London Bridge – train or underground

[1]_The Shard_ is a new building in London. It opened on [2]_____. It is [3]_____ high and it has [4]_____ floors. The designer of the building was [5]_____, an Italian.

I like the Shard because of its shape. It's a bit like a tall, thin, pyramid. It is made of glass and it is beautiful when the sun is shining on it.

The Shard is in [6]_____ in London. It is very close to [7]_____ railway and underground station.

5 Now write a similar description of a building in your country. Make notes first.

Phrases

1 Complete the dialogue with one word in each space.

Paul: Here comes Jethro.

Steve: Oh ¹*no*. What does he want?

Paul: You don't like him, do you?

Steve: No, I don't. He thinks he's better than us because he's so rich.

Paul: That's ²t_____, ³b_____ he is very generous. He bought us all pizza last Friday.

Jethro: Hello.

Paul: Hi. What's up?

Jethro: I've got a slight problem. Can you lend me a ⁴f_____ until tomorrow?

Steve: Five pounds? What ⁵o_____ ⁶e_____ do you need five pounds for?

Vocabulary: Materials

2 ★ Label the picture. Write one word in each space.

1 a pair of r*ubber* boots

2 nice s_____ ties

3 a c_____ box

4 a w_____ statue

5 s _____ jewellery

6 a f_____ hat

7 a d _____ skirt

8 an old l_____ jacket

9 p_____ bags

3 ★★ Complete the sentences with the words from the box.

• cotton • glass • gold • paper
• ~~metals~~ • wool • suede

1 Iron, aluminium and steel are all *metals*.

2 _____ is a soft leather.

3 These windows are made of a strong _____ that is difficult to break.

4 My brother bought his fiancée a beautiful _____ engagement ring.

5 I need some _____ so I can make a jumper for my mum's birthday.

6 This shirt is 100% natural _____.

7 Supermarkets should give customers _____ bags not plastic ones.

Grammar: Present simple passive and past simple passive

4 ★ Complete the sentences with the correct options in capitals.

1 MAKE/ARE MADE

These shirts *are made* in China.

2 GAVE/WERE YOU GIVEN

Who _____ you this hat?

3 SELLS/IS SOLD

A lot of silver jewellery _____ in markets.

4 READ/IS READ

My blog _____ by a hundred people every week.

5 DID THEY ASK/WERE YOU ASKED

What questions _____ in the interview?

6 HEAT/IS HEATED

They _____ the gold until it becomes soft.

5 ⭐⭐ **Complete the sentences with the correct form of the verbs in brackets.**

1 This shirt *was washed* (wash) yesterday.

2 How many plastic bags _____ (throw) away every day?

3 This silk tie _____ (give) to me as a birthday present.

4 How many animals _____ (kill) for their fur every year?

5 My sister _____ (not pay) much money where she works.

6 Why is Peter's name on this book?

   It _____ (not write) by him.

7 Where _____ (you stop) by the police yesterday?

6 ⭐⭐⭐ **Rewrite the underlined sentences with the passive.**

A: I love these earrings.

B: Thanks. ¹Someone made them on Murano near Venice.
   They were made on Murano near Venice.

   It's an island. ²They sent glassmakers there from Venice in 1291.

   Glassmakers _____

   _____.

A: Why?

B: They were worried about fire. ³They still make lots of glass objects there now.

   Lots of glass objects _____

   _____.

   ⁴And thousands of tourists visit the glassmaking factories every year.

   The glassmaking _____

   _____.

A: The colours are beautiful. Are they painted?

B: No. ⁵They colour the glass with gold and other metals.

   The glass _____

   _____.

A: So, have you been to Venice?

B: No. ⁶My aunt gave me these.

   I _____

   _____.

Grammar summary

Present simple passive

Indian clothes **are sold** in the market.

Cotton **isn't grown** in Britain.

Questions	Short answers
Is suede **made** from animal skin?	Yes, it **is**. No it **isn't**.
Are their clothes **sold** online?	Yes, they **are**. No, they **aren't**.
Wh- question	
What are these **used** for?	

Past simple passive

All the glass **was recycled**.

We **weren't given** anything to eat.

Questions	Short answers
Was your computer **checked**?	Yes, it **was**. No it **wasn't**.
Were the factories **shut down**?	Yes, they **were**. No, they **weren't**.
Wh- question	
When were these first **worn**?	

Note

Use

- We use the passive to say what is/was done to a thing or a person.
- We use the passive when:
  - the action or the object is more important than the subject.
    I was given this for my birthday.
  - we don't know the subject.
    The shirt was made in China.
  - we want to talk about a process.
    The clothes are packed into boxes and sent to shops all over the country.

Form

- We form the passive with the correct form of *to be* + the past participle of the verb. The past participle never changes.
- We can use *by* + the subject to say who performed the action. This isn't always necessary.

Common mistakes

~~The jewellery is making in France.~~ ✗
The jewellery is made in France. ✓

5b I couldn't sleep.

Vocabulary: Verbs of action

1 ⭐⭐ **Complete the sentences with the correct form of the verbs from the box. There are three extra verbs.**

> • slip • push • drop • fall • trip • pull
> • float • take off • land • lift • ~~carry~~ • sink

He's ¹*carrying* too many plates. He's going to
² _____ them in a minute.

We ³ _____ an hour ago and, in another half
an hour, we will ⁴ _____.

OK, when you're ready, I'll ⁵ _____ on this
rope and you ⁶ _____.

Look. There's something ⁷ _____ on the
water. Let's try to ⁸ _____ it with these stones.

I can't ⁹ _____ this. It's too heavy.

Grammar: Past ability: *could* and *was/ were able to*

2 ⭐ **Complete the sentences with *could* or *couldn't*. Use the notes.**

When I was six …

✓	✗
1 swim	5 ride a bike
2 read	6 ski
3 write my name	7 cook
4 speak	8 use a computer

When I was six …

1 *I could swim.*
2 _____
3 _____
4 _____
5 _____
6 _____
7 _____
8 _____

3 ⭐⭐ **Replace the underlined words with the correct form of the word in brackets and the main verb.**

1 I <u>couldn't get</u> out of the meeting. (able)
   I *wasn't able to get* out of the meeting.

2 Due to snow, the plane <u>couldn't take</u> off.
   (able)
   Due to snow, the plane
   _____ off.

3 I <u>wasn't able to fix</u> the problem. (could)
   I _____ the problem.

4 <u>Were you able to see</u> anyone? (could)
   _____ anyone?

5 What <u>could you hear</u> outside? (able)
   What _____ outside?

6 We tried, but we <u>couldn't help</u> them. (able)
   We tried, but we _____
   them.

7 <u>Could you swim</u> when you were five? (able)
   _____ when you were
   five?

4 ⭐ Use the prompts to complete the dialogue.

A: We were on holiday in Greece and we wanted to get to an island, but the weather was bad and [1]*the ferry couldn't sail* (ferry/could/sail).

B: Oh no.

A: So, we were stuck in a small town and it was late. [2]_____
(We/not/able/find/a hotel)

B: What did you do?

A: [3]_____
(We/able/go online in a café)

B: And?

A: [4]_____
(So, we/able/look for hotels in Athens)

B: [5]_____
(you/able/find one?)

A: Yes, we were, but it was 35 km away so we took a taxi.

B: Was it expensive?

A: Yes, and when we got to the hotel, my dad realised that he didn't have enough money.
[6]_____
(He/able/pay/the driver)

B: What happened?

A: Luckily there was a bank machine next to the hotel. [7]_____
(He/able/get/some money out)

B: What a night!

Grammar summary

Past ability: *could* and *was/were able to*

Affirmative

He **could** walk from a young age.
She **was able to** escape.
We **were able to** understand the instructions.

Negative

I **couldn't** find the key.
He **wasn't able to** open the door.
They **weren't able to** lift the bags.

Questions	Short answers
Could you see land?	Yes, I **could**.
	No, I **couldn't**.
Was he **able to** finish the test?	Yes, he **was**.
	No, he **wasn't**.
Were they **able to** land the plane?	Yes, they **were**.
	No, they **weren't**.

Wh- question

What could you smell?
How long was she **able to** stay under the water?
How were you **able to** escape?

Note

Use

- We use the positive form of *could* and *was/were able to* for general abilities in the past.
  I could swim when I was three.
  I was able to swim when I was three.
- For a specific ability on one occasion, we use *was/were able to*. We do not use *could*.
  The bag was heavy but he was able to carry it. ✓
  The bag was heavy but he could carry it. ✗
- We can use *could* for specific ability on one occasion when talking about senses (hear, see, smell, taste, feel).
  It was dark but I could see someone in front of me. ✓
- We can use *couldn't* or *wasn't/weren't able to* for general and specific inability in the past.

Form

- We use *could* + the infinitive without *to*.
  We could smell burning.
- We use the correct form of the verb *to be* + *able* + infinitive without *to*.
  They were able to start a fire.

Common mistakes

I could find my phone. ✗
I was able to find my phone. ✓

5c Plato, who was born in Athens, ...

Vocabulary: Landscape and environment

1 ⭐ **Choose the correct options.**

1 There was nothing except sand in the **desert** / forest.

2 The boats are all safe in the **stream** / **harbour**.

3 They walked along a small **path** / **bush**.

4 We washed in a small mountain **ocean** / **stream**.

5 They walked through the **hill** / **valley** between the mountains.

6 There were so many trees in the **forest** / **cliff** that we couldn't find our way.

7 We walked to the top of the **coast** / **hill** and looked at the view.

8 The only thing growing was a small **harbour** / **bush** with yellow flowers.

2 ⭐⭐ **Label the picture. Write one letter in each space.**

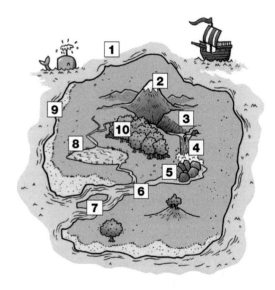

1 *sea*   6 _ _ v _ _
2 _ _ u _ t _ _ n   7 _ s _ _ n _
3 _ _ l _ e _   8 _ _ k _
4 _ _ t _ _ f _ _ l 9 c _ _ _ t
5 _ _ c _ s   10 _ o _ d _

Grammar: Non-defining relative clauses: *who, whose, which, where*

3 ⭐ **Complete the text with the correct pronouns.**

Antillia, [1]*which* is a legendary island in the Atlantic, is also called The Isle of Seven Cities. Portuguese legends say that seven leaders, [2]_____ were escaping from their enemies, landed on the island. They each went to a different part of the island, [3]_____ they built a city.

Zuane Pizzigano, [4]_____ Portolan Chart showed Antillia, was a fifteenth-century map maker. Some people say that Henry the Navigator, [5]_____ father was King John I of Portugal, met people from Antillia. Other people claimed that the island, [6]_____ you could see from Madeira, disappeared when you came close to it.

After 1492, [7]_____ was the year that Columbus reached the 'New World', more and more ships sailed across the Atlantic Ocean. The sailors on these ships, [8]_____ all knew about Antillia, couldn't find the island.

So, did Antillia really exist? Gavin Menzies, [9]_____ is a British writer, says that descriptions of Antillia are exactly like Puerto Rico. So, did the Portuguese cross the Atlantic hundreds of years before Columbus? It's possible.

4 ⭐⭐ **Join the sentences. Use a relative clause.**

1 It was April when we decided to go for a swim in Echo Lake. Echo Lake is 8 km from our town.
It was April when we decided to go for a swim in Echo Lake, which is 8 km from our town.

2 Some friends came too. We knew them from school.
_____

3 We swam to the other side of the lake. Some teenagers were making a fire there.
_____

4 One of my friends had to leave. His parents are strict.
_____

5 The walk home was very tiring. It took a lot longer than the walk there.
_____

Use your English: Give and react to opinions

5 ★ **Complete the dialogues with the words from the box.**

> • opinion • love • agree • true • stand
> • know • sorry • ~~think~~ • mean

1 A: I don't *think* people should wear fur.

  B: I _____.

2 A: In my _____, the coast is the best place to spend the summer.

  B: I _____ what you _____, but I prefer the mountains.

3 A: I can't _____ walking. It's boring.

  B: I'm _____, but I disagree. It's great.

4 A: I _____ swimming. It's brilliant.

  B: That's _____.

6 ★★ **Complete the dialogue with one word in each space.**

Brian: I'm reading a book about the pyramids. Some people think they were made by spacemen.

Alison: I think ¹*so*, too. People couldn't build things like that 5,000 years ago.

Brian: That's ² _____.

Alison: And all the pyramids face the same way.

Brian: I don't ³ _____ so.

Alison: They do. I read about it. I think aliens came to Earth thousands of years ago.

Steve: I'm ⁴ _____ I don't ⁵ _____. I mean, what happened to them?

Alison: ⁶ _____ my opinion, they went back to their planet.

Brian: I think so, ⁷ _____. There are paintings in Peru that look like spacecraft and ancient Mayan texts which talk about 'Men who came from the stars'. How can you explain that?

Steve: Well, I see ⁸ _____ you mean, ⁹ _____ I still don't believe it.

Grammar summary

Non-defining relative clauses: *who, whose, which, where*

People (*who*)
My brother, **who** really annoys me, never washes up.

Possessions (*whose*)
Stella McCartney, **whose** father is Paul McCartney, is a fashion designer.

Things (*which*)
The lost continent of Mu, **which** appears in many legends, probably never existed.

Places (*where*)
The island of Murano, **where** Murano glass comes from, is near Venice.

Note

Use

- We use non-defining relative clauses to give extra, non-essential information about the person, place or thing we are talking about.
  The Metro Centre, which opened last week, is a great place to go shopping.
- The sentence without the non-defining relative clause still makes sense.
  The Metro Centre is a great place to go shopping.

Form

- We separate the non-defining relative clause from the rest of the sentence by commas before and after it.
  Kate Winslett, who is my favourite actress, won an Oscar in 2008.
- We can put the clause at the end of a sentence with a comma before it.
  My friend told me to read Chariots of the Gods, which is a great book.
- We can't use *that* in place of *who* or *which* in non-defining relative clauses.
  We decided to go swimming, which was a really good idea. NOT *We decided to go swimming, that was a really good idea.*

Common mistakes

~~My friend Mark whose dad works in a bank likes tennis.~~ ✗
My friend Mark, whose dad works in a bank, likes tennis. ✓
~~We met on Agistri, where is a really nice island.~~ ✗
We met on Agistri, which is a really nice island. ✓

5 Language round-up

1 Choose the correct options.

1 Mount Etna, **which** / **that** is in Sicily, is over 3,000 metres high.

2 Matt Damon, **who** / **which** played Jason Bourne, is my favourite actor.

3 When we were in Spain we **could** / **were able to** visit Tangier for the day.

4 Madagascar, **where** / **which** is the fourth largest island in the world, is in the Indian Ocean.

5 Pinewood Studios, **which** / **where** a lot of James Bond films are made, are in London.

6 I really wanted to go to the concert, but I **didn't** / **wasn't** able to get a ticket.

7 Joshua Slocum, **that** / **who** sailed round the world, never learned to swim.

8 Liv Tyler, **whose** / **who** father is the singer Steve Tyler, is a great actress.

9 The Titanic, **that** / **which** people said couldn't sink, sank on its first journey.

.../8

2 Complete the texts with one word in each space.

A Playback Clothing make T-shirts and other clothes which ¹*are* all made from recycled materials. The company ²_____ set up by Adam Siskind, ³_____ got the idea after watching a film about the environment. Adam worked with clothes, ⁴_____ meant that he knew a lot about materials. He was ⁵_____ to create clothes from things which ⁶_____ usually thrown away.

B I got these earrings from The Hairy Growler website. They ⁷_____ made from recycled silver. I wasn't able ⁸_____ find anything that I really liked. Then a friend, ⁹_____ mum is a fashion designer, told me about The Hairy Growler. This ring ¹⁰_____ made by them, too. I don't know how they ¹¹_____ able to do it. They're amazing.

.../10

3 Rearrange the letters to make words.

Canada is an amazing country. It is over 7,000 km from St John's, on the ¹*island* (dasiln) of Newfoundland, to Vancouver. The country has the longest ²_____ (toelcaisn) in the world. A lot of the world's fresh water is here in Canada's many ³_____ (aslke) and the country has more ⁴_____ (orsftse) than anywhere except Brazil and Russia. Ships can sail from the Atlantic ⁵_____ (acneo) to the Great Lakes along the St Lawrence ⁶_____ (verir).

.../10

4 Match the questions (1–7) to the answers (a–g). Then write sentences to answer the questions.

1 Who was the Mona Lisa painted by?   *d*

2 Where are kilts worn?   ___

3 Who were you given this scarf by?   ___

4 What is your shirt made of?   ___

5 What could you smell?   ___

6 Are Toyotas made in Korea?   ___

7 Where were the pyramids built?   ___

a) My aunt   e) Egypt

b) Gas   f) Scotland

c) X/Japan   g) Cotton

d) da Vinci

1 *The Mona Lisa was painted by da Vinci.*

2 _____

3 _____

4 _____

5 _____

6 _____

7 _____

.../12

🎧 LISTEN AND CHECK YOUR SCORE

Total	.../40

46

5 Skills practice

SKILLS FOCUS: READING AND WRITING

Read

1 **Read the text and choose the best title.**

A Travelling round the world

B Interesting places close to home

C Cycling round Britain

TRAVEL BLOG

People travel all over the world to see places of outstanding beauty, but there are many places in Britain which are just as beautiful.

Cheddar Gorge is a deep valley with high cliffs on both sides. It attracts half a million people every year. Many of the visitors go to the caves there, where the skeleton of 'Cheddar Man' was found in 1903. The skeleton is about 9,000 years old. The valley is 137 metres deep and Cliff Road, which is popular with cyclists, goes from the valley floor to the top of the cliffs. It's easy to come down, but going up is a real challenge.

Poole Harbour in the south of Britain is as beautiful as Sydney Harbour in Australia. The area used to be a valley which is now under the sea and it has been important for thousands of years. Now it is a popular place for water sports and the many islands in the harbour are home to a large number of birds.

So, next time you want to see somewhere special, why not take a look at what Britain can offer?

2 **Read the text again and answer true (T), false (F) or doesn't say (DS).**

1 The five hundred thousand people who visit Cheddar Gorge are all British. _DS_

2 The skeleton of Cheddar Man is still in the cave there. ___

3 You can only cycle one way on Cliff Road. ___

4 Poole Harbour is more beautiful than Sydney Harbour. ___

5 Many years ago, the area that is now Poole Harbour was not covered by the sea. ___

6 No one lives on the islands in Poole Harbour. ___

Write

3 **Choose the correct options.**

Some friends and I were planning a walk to the top of Snowdon, a mountain in North Wales. [1]**First** / **Finally**, we checked our maps and chose the easiest path and [2]**then / after** we started. It was sunny and we were all excited. We walked past two lakes and stopped for some sandwiches. [3]**Next / After**, we climbed up to a place called Bwlch Glas. That's a Welsh name and I don't know how to say it!

[4]**After / Afterwards** that, we met some walkers coming down the mountain. They said that the weather was getting worse and told us not to go any higher. We wanted to continue but knew that we couldn't so we agreed to go back down the path. [5]**Then / Before that**, we took some photos and promised to return in the summer. As we went down, the rain started. It was very heavy rain and a strong wind. It was difficult to see where we were going and we kept slipping on the wet path. [6]**Then / Finally**, we reached the bottom and ran to a café to get warm and dry. We had soup and hot tea and, [7]**afterwards / next** felt much better. On the train home we fell asleep, tired but happy [8]**afterwards / after** our day out.

4 **Write about a day out which didn't go exactly as you planned. Use the sequencers from Exercise 3 in your story.**

6a It might snow.

Vocabulary: Holidays

1 ★ **Read the text and label the places with the people who stayed there.**

Mr Hanson went on holiday and stayed in a hotel. His children, John and Beth, took a tent. Jenny stayed in a hostel. The Ford family had a week in a caravan and they made friends with The Taylor family, who were in a motorhome. Mr and Mrs Bailey stayed at their favourite Bed and Breakfast accommodation. Mr and Mrs Brown stayed in a cottage on a hill and the Patel family had a self-catering flat near the sea.

1 Mr Hanson
2 _____
3 _____
4 _____
5 _____
6 _____
7 _____
8 _____

2 ★★ **Match the sentences (1–7) to the activities (a–g).**

1 I love cycling, but not on roads.   c

2 I love staying in a tent on holiday.   ___

3 My mum loves going to cities and taking photos of the buildings and famous sights.   ___

4 My sister spends her holidays buying things – clothes, souvenirs, anything!   ___

5 I like going to places where I can learn about the history of the town and look at old clothes, books, coins, etc.   ___

6 When I go to the beach, I don't swim. I just lie on the sand and get brown.   ___

7 We always go to the mountains in the winter. I love coming down really fast.   ___

a) going camping
b) sunbathing
c) going mountain biking
d) going shopping
e) going skiing
f) going to museums
g) sightseeing

Grammar: will/won't/may/might for predictions

3 ★ **Complete the dialogues with one of the words in capitals in each space.**

WILL/WON'T/~~MAY~~

1 A: We should book a hotel room. They ¹*may* be full soon.

B: They ² _____ be full. They never are.

A: Are you sure?

B: Yes. No one goes to the seaside in the winter. There ³ _____ be lots of empty rooms.

WILL/WON'T/MIGHT

2 A: Don't go climbing. You ⁴ _____ fall.

B: Don't worry. I ⁵ _____ fall. Tom's an expert. He ⁶ _____ look after me.

4 ★★ **Complete the text with the phrases from the box.**

- might be • will see • won't have
- won't sleep • won't wait • ~~will be~~

Travel forums

This ¹*will be* our first trip to Sicily. We're travelling on the night train. Any advice?

The train ² _____ a restaurant car so buy some food. Leave a lot of time to catch your plane back because the train ³ _____ late. The plane ⁴ _____ for you! The best thing about the train is that you ⁵ _____ some beautiful views. The worst thing is that you ⁶ _____ very well!

Use your English: Reminders, promises and offers

5 ★★ **Choose the correct options.**

1 A: See you in two weeks.

B: Have a good time. Don't (forget) / **remember** / **worry** to write.

A: Don't **mind** / **worry** / **forget**, I won't.

2 A: I'm going to book the hotel room today.

B: **Don't forget** / **Make sure** / **Would you like** you get rooms with balconies and views of the sea.

A: Don't worry. **I will** / **I won't** / **I would**.

3 A: Oh no!

B: What's wrong?

A: I need to get a guidebook and some maps.

B: **Will you** / **Do you** / **Would you** like me to get them for you? I'm going to the town centre later.

A: Yes, please. That **will** / **would** / **shall** be great.

4 A: The television doesn't work.

B: **Will** / **Shall** / **Would** I tell the man at reception?

A: Don't worry. There's **doesn't matter** / **no need** / **not necessary**. All the programmes are in Greek anyway.

5 A: Are you OK, Tom?

B: No, I'm not. I don't know how to put this tent up.

A: I'll do it for you if **you like** / **you promise** / **you forget**.

B: Really? Thanks.

6 A: Phone us as soon as you arrive.

B: I will. **I promise** / **remember** / **know**.

A: And don't forget to lock your bedroom door when you go out.

B: OK. **I would**. / **If you like**. / **I'll remember**.

Grammar summary

will/won't/may/might for predictions

Affirmative	
I **will/may/might be** late.	
Negative	
They **won't/may not/might not stay** long.	
He **may/might**.	
He **may not/might not**.	
Questions	**Short answers**
Will he **win** the competition?	Yes, he **will**. No, he **won't**.
Wh- questions	
How long **will** the journey **take**?	
It **will/might/may/won't take** a long time.	

Note

Use

- We use the modal auxiliaries *will*, *won't*, *may* and *might* to show how sure we are about future predictions.

- We use *will* and *won't* for predictions we are sure about. Remember, though, that we use *will* for predictions without evidence (see Unit 1a). *The train will/won't be full.*

- We use *may (not)/might (not)* for predictions we are not sure about. *The campsite might/may not be open yet.*

Form

- The form is the same for all persons. We use subject + *will/won't/may (not)/might (not)* + infinitive without *to*.

- We don't usually make questions about predictions using *may* or *might*. *Will the weather be nice?* NOT *Might/May the weather be nice?*

Common mistakes

~~How long we will wait at the airport?~~ ✗
How long will we wait at the airport? ✓

6b If she's here, we'll invite her.

Phrases

1 ⭐ **Complete the dialogues with the phrases from the box.**

• Quick! • Knowing him • obviously
• Who else? • That's him
• How are you doing? • Come on up
---

1 A: Do you think Tom will be here soon?

B: *Knowing him*, he's still asleep in bed.

2 A: Hi, Mark. It's me, Ben.

B: Hi, Ben. I'm just tidying my room.

_____.

3 A: Which one is the instructor?

B: _____ over there. The tall one.

A: _____ Let's talk to him before he leaves.

4 A: Hi, Sally. _____

B: Not bad, thanks. Well, I'm a bit worried about the exam, _____.

A: Me too.

5 A: Is everyone here?

B: We're waiting for one person.

A: Johnny?

B: _____

Grammar: First conditional with *if/unless*; *will* future with *when/as soon as*

2 ⭐ **Match the beginnings (1–8) to the endings (a–h).**

1 If it rains tomorrow,
2 If we can't afford a hotel,
3 If we don't hurry,
4 I'll phone you
5 You'll go very red
6 We'll go windsurfing
7 If you don't listen,
8 I won't invite Hannah

a) we'll stay in a hostel.
b) unless you use sun cream.
c) you won't know what to do.
d) unless she apologises.
e) if the weather is good.
f) as soon as I arrive.
g) I'll stay at home.
h) we'll miss the train.

3 ⭐⭐ **Complete the sentences with *if* or *unless*.**

1 I'll go camping with you *if* you get a better tent.
2 You won't have enough money for a holiday _____ you don't get a job.
3 I won't go to Jack's party _____ he invites my friends.
4 I'll walk to school _____ it's raining.
5 John won't pass his exams _____ he doesn't work harder.
6 My mum will be angry _____ I phone her.

4 ⭐⭐ **Tick (✓) the correct sentences. Correct the incorrect ones.**

1 I'll do my homework as soon as this film will finish.

I'll do my homework as soon as this film finishes.

2 I'll send you an email unless I'm really busy. ✓

_____

3 I'll go to the party unless he sends me an invitation.

_____

4 I'll show you my photos when I will see you.

_____

5 If you're late, I'll wait for you in the café.

_____

6 Will you phone me if your train will be late?

_____

7 I'll go to the concert if the tickets aren't too expensive.

_____

8 What you will do if no one comes to the party?

_____

9 I won't go out unless there isn't something really exciting happening.

_____

10 If Mark doesn't come to my party, I'll be really disappointed.

_____

Vocabulary: Adjectives with prefixes: un-, in- and im-

5 ★ Complete the sentences with the correct prefixes.

1 I don't like camping. Tents are _un_comfortable.

2 I won't go climbing if the leader is ___experienced.

3 I'm too ___fit to go mountain bike riding.

4 The people at the party were really ___friendly.

5 How can you be ___happy in such a beautiful place?

6 I tried windsurfing, but I found it ___possible to stay standing up.

7 It's been raining for six days. Now I know why camping is so ___popular in Scotland!

8 I don't want to go on holiday with my parents. I want to be completely ___dependent this year.

6 ★★ Complete the sentences with the correct form of the adjectives from the box.

- ~~healthy~~ • attractive • likely • necessary
- formal • tidy • interesting • patient

1 Don't eat too much _unhealthy_ food when you go on holiday.

2 I love hotels. You can leave your room _____ in the morning and it will be perfect again when you get back.

3 We always eat in restaurants on holiday so a kitchen is _____.

4 'Come on train, come on, hurry up.' ' Don't be so _____. Relax and enjoy the sunshine.'

5 The beach and the harbour are pretty, but the town is very _____ with all these ugly buildings.

6 The museum was really _____ – there was nothing much in it at all.

7 It's a five star hotel, but it's quite _____. You don't need to wear a tie or anything like that!

8 I might have a party, but it's very _____ I'm afraid. My mum is really against the idea.

Grammar summary

First conditional with if/unless

Affirmative
They **will arrive** soon **if** the train **is** on time.
They **will arrive** soon **unless** the train **is** late.

Negative
We **won't enjoy** the party **if there isn't** any music.
We **won't enjoy** the party **unless there is** some music.

Questions	Short answers
Will you **go** cycling **if** the weather **is** nice?	Yes, I **will**. No, I **won't**.

Wh- questions
Who **will** you **invite if** you **have** a party?

Note

Use
- We use the first conditional with if and unless to talk about the result of a possible future event.
- We use unless for a result that does not happen.

Form
- We use if/unless + present simple for the possible future event and will + infinitive without to for the result.
- When we start with the if/unless part of the sentence, we use a comma.
  Unless you apologise, I won't go out with you again.
- When we start with the result, we don't use a comma.

Common mistakes
~~I'll wait for you unless I don't hear from you.~~ ✗
I'll wait for you unless I hear from you. ✓

will future with when/as soon as

I'll phone when/as soon as the plane lands.	
Questions	**Short answers**
Will you **start** work **as soon as** you **get** home?	Yes, I **will**. No, I **won't**.
Wh- questions	
What **will** you **say** when you see Greg?	

Note

Use
- We use the will future with when/as soon as to show that one thing will happen very soon after another.

Form
- We follow the same rules as for the first conditional.

Common mistakes
~~When I will arrive, I'll phone you.~~ ✗
When I arrive, I'll phone you. ✓

6c The two men hadn't met before.

Vocabulary: Collocations with *lose*

1 ★ **Match the beginnings (1–7) to the endings (a–g).**

1 I hope we don't lose   c

2 Paul is upset because his team lost   ___

3 Jake gets very excited about new hobbies, but then he loses   ___

4 If you eat crisps every day, you'll never lose ___

5 I saw Ben windsurfing for a few minutes, but then I lost   ___

6 If we don't follow the path, we might lose   ___

7 If I tell you what I did wrong, please don't lose   ___

a) interest quickly.

b) our way.

c) touch when you go to university.

d) sight of him.

e) your temper.

f) weight.

g) an important match.

2 ★★ **Complete the sentences with the correct form of the collocations from the box.**

> • lose interest • lose sight of • lose weight
> • lose (one's) memory • lose a match
> • lose (one's) temper • lose touch with

1 We haven't *lost a match* since last year when Park school won 3–1.

2 I'm going to _____ before I go to the beach this year. At least 3 kgs.

3 I think I'm _____. I can't remember why I came to the living room.

4 I _____ in this book on page 3. It was so boring.

5 When my dad _____, he shouts at us for no reason.

6 I _____ my best friend when she moved to New Zealand.

7 We stayed close together because we didn't want to _____ each other in the fog.

Grammar: Past perfect simple

3 ★ **Complete the sentences with the phrases from the box.**

> • I hadn't studied for it • we hadn't put
> it up properly • we hadn't slept all night
> • someone had put salt in it • he hadn't eaten
> anything • we hadn't done our projects

1 I failed the exam because *I hadn't studied for it*.

2 We were tired because

_____.

3 Mark was hungry because

_____.

4 Our teacher was upset because

_____.

5 Our tent fell down because

_____.

6 We couldn't drink our tea because

_____.

4 ★★ **Complete the text with the past perfect simple form of the verbs in brackets.**

Sarah Ho and Wilson Ng got married in 2012. They [1]*had been* (be) friends when they were young children in Britain, but they [2]_____ (lose) touch when Wilson's family moved to America. Sarah [3]_____ (never forget) Wilson, though.

Twenty-three years later, they met up again in London. Sarah [4]_____ (ask) her mother for Wilson's phone number and she [5]_____ (send) him a text. Sarah then decided to visit him in the USA but, before she could organise a trip, Wilson [6]_____ (come) to Britain. They both realised that they were in love. Neither of them [7]_____ (meet) anyone else that they cared about so much.

Wilson returned to the USA but, two months later, he was back in Britain with an engagement ring. When he asked Sarah to marry him, she said 'Yes' and the real life fairy tale came true.

5 ★★★ **Make questions and statements. Use the prompts and the past perfect simple.**

In 1926, Agatha Christie disappeared. Why?

¹She/have/argument/husband

She had had an argument with her

husband. ²He/fall/love/another woman.

_____

On the day Agatha Christie disappeared

³he/tell/her/wanted/get divorced.

_____

Agatha Christie drove away from her home and, later that day, her car was found. ⁴She/ leave/her driving licence/some clothes/in/car.

_____

⁵But where/she/go? _____

⁶she/kill/herself? _____

No one knew.

1,000 police officers and 15,000 volunteers spent days looking for Agatha. Then, ten days later, she was found in a hotel in Harrogate, Yorkshire.

⁷She/book/in as Mrs Teresa Neele from South

Africa. _____

⁸No one/recognise/her. _____

⁹Why/she/do/it? _____

¹⁰How/she/get there without her car?

_____

Agatha Christie never told anyone and no one ever found out.

Grammar summary

Past perfect simple

Affirmative	
I **had forgotten** to lock the front door.	
Negative	
They **hadn't been** in contact for a long time.	
Questions	**Short answers**
Had I said the wrong thing?	Yes, I **had**.
	No, I **hadn't**.
Wh- questions	
Where **had I seen** that face before?	

Note

Use

- We use the past perfect simple to say that something happened before another past event.
  When I arrived, everyone had left. (They left before I arrived.)
- We don't use the past perfect simple when it is obvious which order the things happened in.
  Everyone left and then I arrived. NOT *Everyone had left and then I arrived.*

Form

- The form is the same for all persons. In affirmative sentences, we use *had* + the past participle.
  We had been there before.
- In negatives, we use *hadn't* + the past participle.
  When I got into the exam, I realised I hadn't studied enough.
- In questions, we use *Had* + the subject + the past participle.
  Had you ever met Julia before the party last week?

Common mistakes

~~*I hadn't went there before.*~~ ✗
I hadn't been there before. ✓
~~*He had read the letter when you saw him?*~~ ✗
Had he read the letter when you saw him? ✓

6 Language round-up

1 Complete the texts with the words from the box. There are three extra words.

> • will • If • been • when • Unless • temper
> • I'll • might • soon

Hi Mike,
I got the summer job I told you about. It [1]*will* be strange to work during the holidays.
Andy

Well, it wasn't the best day I've ever had! The boss loses his [2]_____ very quickly and for no real reason. [3]_____ he shouts like that every day, I [4]_____ not stay there much longer. [5]_____ things change, I don't think [6]_____ be there next week.
Andy

I lost my job yesterday because I shouted at the boss. Maybe we can go camping somewhere?
Andy

.../10

2 Complete the dialogue with one word in each space.

Beth: Are you [1]*going* camping?

Helen: No way. I'm not sleeping in a [2]t_____ again! I'm staying in a [3]s_____-catering flat with Teresa.

Beth: Teresa! Wow! I lost [4]t_____ with her when she moved to Devon.

Helen: So did I but I found out that Melanie had contacted Teresa.

Beth: Well, I'm going to Wales with my parents. And I'll [5]s_____ in the sea and I'll [6]p_____ beach volleyball. That's great fun.

.../10

3 Complete the second sentence so that it has the same meaning as the first. Use the word in capitals.

1 It was the first time Ellie had met Matt. HADN'T
Ellie *hadn't met Matt* before that.

2 It's possible that I won't be on time. MIGHT
I _____ on time.

3 The party finished and then Ben arrived. HAD
By the time Ben _____ finished.

4 I got bored after an hour. INTEREST
I _____ after an hour.

5 I'll go to the cinema unless we get a lot of homework. DON'T
_____ a lot of homework, I'll go to the cinema.

6 When I know my results, I'll phone you. SOON
I'll phone you _____ my results.

.../10

4 Complete the dialogue with the correct form of the words from the box.

> • likely • friendly • necessary • be
> • write • possible

A: Why are your neighbours so [1]*unfriendly*?

B: I don't know. We've tried but it's [2]_____ to make them happy. Last week, they complained about my party. We'd [3]_____ them a note to explain and they said it was OK. Then they just rang the police. It really was [4]_____.

A: What did the police do?

B: They were fine. They said there had [5]_____ some difficult situations before. Dad thinks we can be friends, but I think it's very [6]_____.

.../10

🎧 **LISTEN AND CHECK YOUR SCORE**	
Total	.../40

6 Skills practice

SKILLS FOCUS: READING, LISTENING AND WRITING

Read

1 Read the text and choose the best ending.

a) Why me?   b) Why him?   c) Why now?

Terry had known Julie for years. They had been in their first class together. They were still friends but, while Terry loved Julie, she saw him as just a friend. He was never brave enough to tell her the truth. She even asked him for advice when she and her boyfriend, Alan, had arguments.

In April, Terry went on an exchange trip to France and was staying with a boy called Alain! The family were nice and Alain's sister, Simone, was just a year younger than Terry and beautiful. Terry spoke a lot of French. Not so much to Alain, although they got on quite well, but mainly to Simone. They talked about everything and seemed to like exactly the same things.

By the time he got back to England, Terry wanted to tell Julie all about Simone. He rang her up and they arranged to meet. When he saw her, Terry told her that he had some big news to tell her. 'Me too,' said Julie. 'I've broken up with Alan. I suddenly realised that it was you I loved. I didn't know until you went away. I really missed you.' Julie smiled and looked at Terry. Terry sat there and thought, sadly: ___

2 Read the text again and choose the correct options.

1 Terry and Julie had been **friends / boyfriend and girlfriend** for a long time.

2 Julie **knew / didn't know** how Terry felt about her.

3 Simone was **Alan's / Alain's** sister.

4 Terry was **older / younger** than Simone.

5 Alain and Terry **didn't get on well / got on quite well**.

6 When Terry got home, he rang **Julie / Simone**.

7 Julie broke up with Alan because **he went away / she realised she loved someone else**.

Listen

3 🎧 Listen to the conversation and choose the correct options.

1 What time did they arrive at the cottage? **Six o'clock / Seven o'clock**

2 What did Cathy's dad find in the kitchen? **Cheese and juice / Tea and coffee**

3 What is the temperature now? **20°C / 25°C**

4 🎧 Listen again and answer the questions.

1 What kind of accommodation are they staying in? It's a _cottage_.

2 What did the man at the cottage do? He _____.

3 How far away from the sea are they? They are _____.

4 What is Cathy wearing at the moment? She's _____.

5 What kind of holiday is Rob going on? He's _____.

Write

5 Use the notes to write a more interesting paragraph about a holiday.

We arrived at our hotel. (1) Then we went out to see the town. (2) We went to a restaurant. (3) Now we're back in the hotel. I'm in my room. (4) Tomorrow I think we'll go to the beach. (5)

1 When did you arrive? What's the hotel like? Describe the room. What was the first thing you did when you arrived?

2 Is the town pleasant? What's the weather like? What did you see in the town?

3 What did you eat or drink in the restaurant? Did you try any local food? What did you think of it?

4 How do you feel now? What are you going to do when you finish writing?

5 What will you do on the beach? What will you do if the weather isn't very good?

We arrived at our hotel at five o'clock this afternoon. It's a modern hotel and very comfortable. Our room ...

7a He told her to throw it.

Grammar: Reported requests and commands

1 ⭐ **Put the verbs in brackets into the correct affirmative (✓) or negative (✗) form.**

Our teacher …

1 asked us *to bring* (✓ bring) some food for a picnic.

2 told us _____ (✓ wear) warm clothes.

3 told us _____ (✗ be) late.

My mum …

4 asked me _____ (✓ buy) some bread.

5 told me _____ (✗ talk) to any strangers.

6 asked me _____ (✓ cook) dinner.

I …

7 asked my dad _____ (✓ take) me to school.

8 told my brother _____ (✗ go) into my room.

9 asked my mum _____ (✗ phone) me at school.

2 ⭐⭐ **Write what the people actually said.**

1 Mum told me to lay the table.

(*Lay the table.*)

2 Dad told me to be quiet.

(_____)

3 Mark told me not to use his computer.

(_____)

4 Our teacher told us not to talk during the exam.

(_____)

5 My friend told me to phone her at 6 p.m.

(_____)

6 My dad told me to do my schoolwork.

(_____)

3 ⭐⭐ **Complete the text with the correct form of the verbs from the box.**

> • give • ~~help~~ • not talk • buy • be
> • listen • meet • look • not be

My friend had a job interview last week. Before the interview, she asked me [1]*to help* her choose some clothes. I told her [2]_____ me outside the big clothes shop in Oxford Road and I told her [3]_____ late. When she arrived – 20 minutes late – we went into the shop. She was looking at jeans, but I told her [4]_____ a dress or a skirt. She found a nice, blue dress and we went for a coffee. She asked me [5]_____ her some advice as she'd never had a job interview before. I told her [6]_____ into the interviewer's eyes and [7]_____ friendly and natural. I told her [8]_____ carefully to the questions and [9]_____ about unimportant things like boyfriends and pop music!

I think she listened to my advice because she got the job.

4 ⭐⭐⭐ **Rewrite the sentences as reported requests and commands.**

1 (My friend to me) Don't go outside.

   My friend told me not to go outside.

2 (My brother to me) Can you help me with my homework?

   _____

3 (Me to David) Go away!

   _____

4 (My mum to my sister) Hurry up!

   _____

5 (Our teacher to us) Don't look at the answers.

   _____

6 (My mum to my brother) Switch off your computer.

   _____

Vocabulary: Adjective word order

5 ⭐ **Use the information in the sentences to make one sentence.**

1 The car is American. The car is new. The car is expensive. The car is brown.

It's *an expensive new brown American car*.

2 Venice is beautiful. Venice is Italian. Venice is old. Venice is a city.

Venice _____.

3 Kangaroos are animals. Kangaroos are brown. Kangaroos are strange. Kangaroos are Australian.

Kangaroos _____.

4 The lantern is Chinese. The lantern is made of glass. The lantern is pretty. The lantern is small.

It _____.

Grammar summary

Reported requests and commands

Direct speech	Reported speech
Affirmative	
Hurry up. Can you help me?	He **told** us **to hurry** up. He **asked** me **to help** him.
Negative	
Don't make a noise. Please don't eat my chips.	They **told** us **not to make** a noise. She **asked** me **not to eat** her chips.

Note

Use
- We use reported requests and commands to report what someone asked or told another person to do.
- We use *ask* in requests and *tell* in commands.
  She asked me to walk more slowly.
  They told us to go away.

Form
- To report a polite request, we use the subject + *asked* + object and *(+ not)* + infinitive.
  They asked us to come in.
- To report a command, we use subject + *told* + object *(+ not)* + infinitive
  I told them to play their music more quietly.
  I told him not to drive so fast.

Common mistakes
~~She told me to not be so mean.~~ ✗
She told me not to be so mean. ✓
~~They asked us sing a song.~~ ✗
They asked us to sing a song. ✓

7b He said he was writing a book.

Grammar: Reported statements

1 ⭐ **Look at the quiz and complete the dialogue with the correct verb forms.**

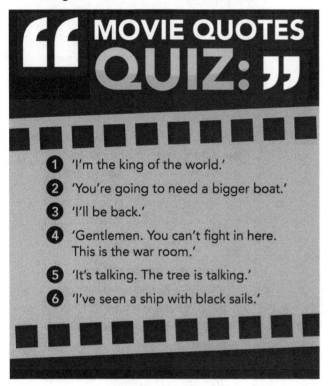

" MOVIE QUOTES QUIZ: "

1. 'I'm the king of the world.'
2. 'You're going to need a bigger boat.'
3. 'I'll be back.'
4. 'Gentlemen. You can't fight in here. This is the war room.'
5. 'It's talking. The tree is talking.'
6. 'I've seen a ship with black sails.'

A: OK, I know the first one. Leonardo DiCaprio said he ¹_was_ the king of the world in *Titanic*. And I remember number 2. It was in *Jaws*. The policeman told the fisherman that he ²_____ a bigger boat when he first saw the shark.

B: I've never seen *Jaws*. Number 3 is my favourite. *The Terminator*, Arnold Schwarzenegger, said that he ³_____ back.

A: So, number 4. Someone said that the men ⁴_____ in the room because it was the war room. It sounds like a comedy.

B: Oh, I know. *Dr Strangelove*.

A: I've never even heard of that! The last two are easy. Pippin said that the tree ⁵_____ in *The Lord of the Rings* and one of the pirates said that he ⁶_____ a ship with black sails in one of the *Pirates of the Caribbean* films.

B: Brilliant. We've finished.

2 ⭐⭐ **Complete the reported statements.**

1. Emily: 'I love camping.'
   Emily said that _she loved camping_.
2. Jack: 'I haven't tried windsurfing.'
   Jack said that _____.
3. Eliza: 'I'll be in London soon.'
   Eliza said that _____.
4. My parents: 'The dentist is waiting for you.'
   My parents told me that

   _____.
5. Melanie: 'We didn't do anything interesting.'
   Melanie said that _____.
6. Paolo: 'I'm going to learn Spanish.'
   Paolo said that _____.

3 ⭐⭐⭐ **Read the message. Then complete the text in reported speech.**

> Hi, Kate. It's Nathan. Listen. I was in Mr McGarry's classroom just now and I saw our exam results on his desk. Alison will be happy. She got 94%. My mum's going to be very angry. I failed. I'm going home now. I'll wash up and cook dinner and then my mum will be in a good mood when I tell her. See you later.

I got a message from Nathan earlier. He said that ¹_he'd been_ in Mr McGarry's classroom and ²_____ our exam results. He told me that Alison ³_____ because ⁴_____ 94% in the exam. He also said that his mum ⁵_____ very angry because ⁶_____ the exam. He told me that ⁷_____ home and that ⁸_____ and cook dinner and then his mother ⁹_____ in a good mood when he told her. Poor old Nathan.

Vocabulary: Appearance

4 ★ **Complete the dialogue with the answers from the box.**

- Square. • Middle-aged. • No, quite thin.
- No, but he had a moustache.
- It was blond. • ~~He was bald.~~
- She had a fringe. • Yes, very. And straight.

A: There were two people, a man and a woman.

B: Tell me about the man. Can you describe his hair?

A: Hair? He hadn't got any hair. ¹*He was bald.*

B: How old was he?

A: I don't know. Forty or fifty. ² _____

B: What shape was his face?

A: ³ _____

B: Was he overweight?

A: ⁴ _____

B: Did he have a beard?

A: ⁵ _____

B: OK, now the woman. What colour was her hair?

A: ⁶ _____

B: Was it long?

A: ⁷ _____

B: Can you tell me anything else about her hair?

A: ⁸ _____

B: OK, thank you. That's very helpful.

5 ★★ **Complete the description words with one letter in each space.**

This is my brother. He's in his early ¹*twenties.* He's got ²s _ _ r _, ³s _ _ k _ hair and he wears ⁴g _ _ s _ _ _. He's got a ⁵s _ _ _ r _ face. He's quite ⁶s _ _ m (even thin) some girls think he's good-looking.

This is me. I'm in my ⁷t _ _ n _. I've got ⁸l _ _ _, ⁹w _ _ y, blond hair with a ¹⁰p _ _ t _ _ g on the side. I've got big, brown ¹¹e _ e _ and a ¹²r _ _ n _ face. I'm ¹³m _ d _ _ m–h _ _ g _ t.

Grammar summary

Reported statements

Direct statement	Reported statement
I **live** in London.	He **said (that) he lived** in London.
We**'ve been** to Scotland.	She **said (that) they had been** to Scotland.
I**'ll help** you.	He **told me (that) he would help** me.

Note

Use

- We use reported statements to report what someone has said.

Form

- When we change a direct statement into a reported one, we usually 'move the tense back'.
  Present simple → *past simple*
  Present continuous → *past continuous*
  Past simple → *past perfect*
  Present perfect → *past perfect*
  will → *would*, *can* → *could*, *may* → *might*
- Past perfect, *could*, *would* and *might* do not 'go back' in reported statements.
  I would love to see you. → *He said that he would love to see us.*
- We often need to change subject and object pronouns.
  I love you → *Mark told me that he loved me.*
- We often need to change possessive adjectives.
  You've got my phone. → *Jenny told me that I had got her phone.*
- To form reported statements, we can use *said* or *told*. When we use *told*, we always use a direct object without *to*. After *said*, we can use *to* + direct object or we can write the sentence with no object.
  He told me that I was late. ✓
  He said that I was late. ✓
  He said to me that I was late. ✓
  ~~*He told that I was late.*~~ ✗
  ~~*He said me that I was late.*~~ ✗
  ~~*He told to me that I was late.*~~ ✗
- We often miss out *that* in informal writing and speech.
  They told us the train had gone.

Common mistakes
~~*He said that our friends have left.*~~ ✗
He said that our friends had left. ✓

7c She asked if I could come …

Phrases

1 ★ **Complete the dialogue with the words from the box.**

> • Just • hard • can't • ~~so~~ • minute • think
> • luck • excited

A: Oh, I'm ¹so ²_____! I love quizzes.

B: OK, everybody. Quiet now. Question one. Who said: 'My horse, my horse, my kingdom for a horse?'

A: Oh, I know this one. ³_____ a ⁴_____.
Oh, it's … it's Shakespeare. Wait. Oh no! I
⁵_____ ⁶_____. Er … Was it Henry V?

B: No, ⁷_____ ⁸_____. It was Richard III.

Grammar: Reported questions

2 ★ **Choose the correct options.**

1 'How are you?'
Ben asked how **was I** / **I was**.

2 'Where are you going?'
They asked me where **am I** / **I was** going.

3 'Do you like sunbathing?'
I asked Jemima **if she liked** / **did she like** sunbathing.

4 'Where does your mum work?'
My teacher asked me where **did my mum work** / **my mum worked**.

5 'Where have you been?'
They asked us where **we had been** / **had we been**.

6 'How much does the dress cost?'
The girl asked the shop assistant how much **the dress cost** / **cost the dress**.

7 'Will you be ready soon?'
My mum asked my dad **would he be** / **if he would be** ready soon.

8 'Why did you go to Margate on holiday?'
My friend asked me why **I had gone** / **had I gone** to Margate on holiday.

3 ★★ **Correct the sentences.**

1 She asked was I English.
She asked if I was English.

2 They asked us where do we work.

_____

3 She asked me what was my name.

_____

4 He asked her why had she gone home so early.

_____

5 I asked him did he know Kate Simmons.

_____

6 My dad asked us why hadn't we done our homework.

_____

4 ★★★ **Read the dialogue. Then complete the reported questions in the text.**

A: Hi, what's happening?

B: There's a fire.

A: I can see that. How did it start?

B: I don't know. I was at the shops.

A: Is there anyone in the house?

B: No, there isn't. The children are at school.

A: Can we take some photos?

B: You'll have to ask the firemen.

There was a small fire yesterday at a house in Latimer Street. I asked the owner of the house ¹*what was happening*. She was in shock and told me that there was a fire. I asked her ²_____, but she didn't know. She had been at the shops. Then I asked her ³_____, but luckily there wasn't. She told me that the children were at school. Finally, I asked her ⁴_____, but she told us to ask a fireman.

Use your English: Speak on the phone

5 ⭐ **Complete the phone calls with the phrases from the box.**

- Can I take a message? • Hang on.
- ~~Is Lucy there?~~ • Who's calling, please?
- I'm afraid she's out. • It's Mandy.

1 Jack: Hello.

Tom: Hi. It's Tom here. *Is Lucy there?*

Jack: Oh, hello, Tom. I'm sorry.

_____.

_____.

Tom: Yes, please. Can you tell her I phoned?

Jack: OK, no problem.

2 Mandy: Hello, is Rebecca there?

Mrs Green: _____.

Mandy: _____.

Mrs Green: Oh, hello, Mandy.

_____. I'll get her.

Mandy: Thanks.

6 ⭐⭐ **Complete the dialogues with one word in each space.**

1 John: Hello. Can I s*peak* to Debbie, please?

Alex: Who's c_____?

John: It's John.

Alex: Oh, hello, John. J_____ a m_____. Debbie's upstairs doing her homework. I'll g_____ her.

John: Thank you.

2 Dan: Hello. Dan s_____.

Simon: Oh, hi, Dan. T_____ is Simon. Is Amelia t_____?

Dan: No, I'm s _____. She's o_____. She won't be back until about ten o'clock. Can I t_____ a m_____?

Simon: It's OK. I'll call again tomorrow. Bye.

Grammar summary

Reported questions

Wh- questions

Direct questions	Reported questions
Who **does** Martin **love**?	She **asked** who Martin **loved**.
Where **did** you **go**?	He **asked me** where I **had been**.
How tall **is** he?	I **asked** how tall he **was**.
When **will** you **do** your homework?	My mum **asked me** when I **would do** my homework.

Yes/No questions

Direct questions	Reported questions
Are you French?	I **asked him if** he **was** French.
Did you **eat** lunch?	She **asked me if** I **had eaten** lunch.
Have you **been** to Rome?	He **asked us if** we **had been** to Rome.
Can you swim?	We **asked her if** she **could** swim.

Note

Use

- We use reported questions to report what someone has asked.

Form

We use the same tense, pronoun and possessive adjective changes as for reported statements.

How do you get to school? → *He asked me how I got to school.*

- In *Wh-* questions, we use *asked* + (object) + question word + subject + verb. We don't use a question mark at the end of the reported question.
  Where were you earlier? → *She asked me where I had been earlier.*
- We don't use the auxiliary verb *do/does/did* in reported questions.
  Where do you live? He asked us where we lived. NOT ~~*He asked us where did we live.*~~
- In *Yes/No* questions, we use *asked* + (object) + *if* + subject + verb. We don't use the auxiliary verbs *do/does/did.*
  They asked us if we knew the way to Manchester.
  He asked if I had finished my homework.

Common mistakes

~~He asked if I did speak French.~~ ✗
He asked if I spoke French. ✓
~~They asked us where had we been.~~ ✗
They asked us where we had been. ✓

7 Language round-up

1 Complete the table with the words from the box.

- enormous • horrible • parting • Mexican
- modern • fair • blond • fringe
- overweight • round • slim • square
- teenage • ~~large~~ • weird • Spanish

Size	Age
large	_____
_____	_____
Origin	**Hair style**
_____	_____
_____	_____
Opinion	**Shape**
_____	_____
_____	_____
Hair colour	**Build**
_____	_____
_____	_____

.../15

2 Complete the text with one word in each space.

I had a job interview yesterday. The interviewer, who was middle-[1]*aged*, asked me lots of questions. She asked [2]_____ I had ever worked in a shop before. I [3]_____ her that I hadn't, but that I had [4]_____ a waitress last summer. Then she asked [5]_____ about my school, what I wanted to do in the future and what I [6]_____ in my free time.

My mum had told me [7]_____ to be late. In the end, I got there twenty minutes early. There was a boy waiting there for an interview. He was about eighteen with medium-[8]_____ hair. He was very good-[9]_____ and well-[10]_____. He asked me [11]_____ give him my phone number. I didn't, but I [12]_____ him my name and he sent me a Facebook friend request!

.../11

3 Complete the reported statements, questions and commands.

1 'Finish your dinner.'

My dad told me *to finish my dinner*.

2 'Don't worry about your exams.'

My friend told me _____

_____.

3 'You're driving too fast.'

My mum told my dad that

_____.

4 'I don't like pizza.'

My friend, Sara, told me that

_____.

5 'Do you often eat fast food?'

My cousin asked me _____.

6 'Have you read *The Lord of the Rings*?'

I asked Mrs Green _____

_____.

7 'My watch has stopped.'

My sister said that _____.

.../6

4 Complete the sentences with the correct form of the words in capitals.

1 Gemma is very *attractive*.	ATTRACT
2 My sister is in her early _____.	TWENTY
3 Meg's got long, _____ hair.	WAVE
4 Paolo is an _____ boy from Genoa.	ITALY
5 You wear very _____ clothes!	COLOUR
6 Mum doesn't like my _____ hair.	SPIKE
7 It's _____ to speak a foreign language.	USE
8 That's a really _____ dress.	BEAUTY
9 There are two _____ students in our class.	CHINA

.../8

🎧 **LISTEN AND CHECK YOUR SCORE**

Total	.../40

7 Skills practice

SKILLS FOCUS: READING AND WRITING

Read

1 Read the text and complete the sentences with the correct name.

1 *Frank Kaufman* worked for the army.

2 _____ said that the alien's eyes were larger than a human's.

3 _____ went to the moon.

4 _____ described the colour of the aliens' uniforms.

5 _____ mentioned the number of aliens he had seen.

6 _____ has seen secret information about the aliens.

UNSOLVED!

Mysteries > Aliens > Roswell

In 1947, the town of Roswell in New Mexico, became famous when several people said that they had seen an alien spacecraft crash in the area. Did it really happen? In an interview in 1993, Frank Kaufmann said that he had worked for the army and that he had seen four dead aliens. They were wearing uniforms and were like small humans. They were about 1.60 metres tall and their eyes, noses and ears were smaller than a human's. They were completely hairless with grey skin. Another man, Thomas Gonzales, said that he had also seen the aliens. He talked about silver uniforms and grey skin but he said that their eyes were bigger than a human's.

Edgar Mitchell, who walked on the moon in 1971 when he was a part of the Apollo 14 team, said that he had seen secret documents about Roswell. He said that the government had known about the crash and that scientists had examined the alien bodies.

So, is the story true or not? One day, we may find out.

Write

2 Choose the correct options to complete the letter.

> 1_____ Mrs Taylor,
>
> 2_____ you very much
>
> 3_____ helping me with my summer job at your newspaper. It was very kind of you to teach me so much about the newspaper business.
>
> I'm very sorry that I haven't written before now, 4_____ the new term at school has been very busy.
>
> Thank you again for all your help. I hope I can work with you again next summer.
>
> With best 5_____,
> Laura Davies
>
> 6_____ Good luck 7_____ your new look online pages. I'm sure they'll be very successful.

1 (a) Dear   b) Hi   c) Hello

2 a) Cheers   b) Thanks   c) Thank

3 a) to   b) with   c) for

4 a) but   b) because   c) while

5 a) love   b) wishes   c) time

6 a) B.S.   b) P.S.   c) P.B.

7 a) from   b) to   c) with

3 Look at the notes below and write a thank you letter.

Roy Slade, a local musician, came to see you and your friends practising. He gave you some ideas and helped you to find a club where you could play a concert. Write him a thank you letter.

- Thank him and tell him how the concert went.

- Apologise for not writing sooner and tell him why.

- At the end of the letter, add a message of good luck with his new album and tell him you are looking forward to hearing it.

8a How would you feel?

Grammar: Second conditional

1 ★ **Match the beginnings (1–8) to the endings (a–h.)**

1 If Mark was here   _b_

2 Where would your dad work ___

3 My parents would buy a new car ___

4 If we had a mobile phone ___

5 If the sea was warmer   ___

6 Would you enjoy cricket more ___

7 What would you wear   ___

8 My dad would be amazed ___

a) if I explained the rules to you?

b) he would know what to do.

c) if they had more money.

d) if he wasn't a doctor?

e) if you had a job interview tomorrow?

f) if he could see me now.

g) I'd go for a swim.

h) we could phone your parents.

2 ★★ **Complete the sentences with the correct form of the verbs in brackets.**

1 If I _had_ (have) more money, I _would buy_ (buy) a new computer.

2 If we _____ (not have) an exam tomorrow, I _____ (go) out this evening.

3 What _____ (you do) if you _____ (be) me?

4 If you _____ (have) the chance, _____ (you want) to be famous?

5 If the internet _____ (stop) working, you _____ (not know) what to do.

6 Where _____ (you go) if you _____ (can) choose?

7 _____ (your neighbours be) angry if we _____ (have) a party at your house?

8 What _____ (your parents say) if you _____ (decide) to move to another country?

3 ★★ **Read the situations then complete the conditional sentences.**

1 There's nothing to do so I'm bored.

If there _was something_ to do, I _wouldn't be_ bored.

2 This exercise is difficult so I can't do it.

If this exercise _____, _____ it.

3 There isn't enough wind so we can't go windsurfing.

If _____ more wind, _____ windsurfing.

4 The concert tickets are very expensive so we aren't going.

We _____ to the concert _____ so expensive.

5 I don't understand French so my parents want me to go to extra lessons.

If _____ French, my parents _____ to go to extra lessons.

4 ★★★ **Use the prompts to write questions.**

1 What/you do/this evening/be/no electricity in your house?

What would you do this evening if there was no electricity in your house?

2 someone/make/a film of your life/who/play/you?

_____

3 someone/offer/you a job in Australia/you go?

_____

4 What/you say/your friends/ask/you to go camping this summer?

_____

5 Which photo/you keep/you/can/only keep one?

_____

6 If/you/have/a blog/what/you write/about?

_____

Vocabulary: -ed and -ing adjectives

5 ★ **Complete the sentences with the correct form of the words in capitals.**

1 AMAZE

Paul was _amazed_ when he saw his exam paper. 98%! That was an _amazing_ result.

2 INTEREST

I'm not usually _____ in museums but some of the things in here are very

_____.

3 FRIGHTEN

The film was very _____. Sam slept with his light on that night because he was _____.

4 BORE

The lesson isn't _____. If you took part in the discussion, you wouldn't be

_____.

5 DISAPPOINT

It was a _____ result. We knew they were a good team, but we are all _____ to lose 8–1.

6 ANNOY

My brother is very _____. I was really _____ with him when he broke my phone.

6 ★★ **Complete the sentences with the correct form of the words from the box.**

• excite • amuse • tire • shock • ~~frighten~~

1 'What's that game?' 'It's a new horror game. It's really _frightening_.'

2 'What did you think of the comedy film?' 'It was quite _____, but I didn't laugh much.'

3 Why are you so _____? Did you go to bed late last night?

4 We were all _____ when the teacher said that the whole class had failed the exam.

5 It has been very _____ here with a concert on Friday and a big storm on Saturday night.

Grammar summary

Second conditional

Affirmative
I **would go** to the concert **if** it **was** on at the weekend.
If we **lived** near the mountains, we **would go** skiing every weekend.

Negative
I **wouldn't watch** this programme **if** there **was** something else to do.
If she **didn't like** the food, she **wouldn't eat** it.

Questions
Would you **cheat** in an exam **if** you **didn't know** the answers?

Short answers
Yes, I **would**.
No, I **wouldn't**.

Wh- questions:
What **would** you **do if** your parents **decided** to move to a different town?

Note

Use

- We use the second conditional to talk about the result of an unlikely or impossible situation in the present or future.

   If I were you, I'd wear these black jeans.

   If I didn't go to university, my parents would be disappointed.

Form

- There are two parts in a second conditional sentence. We use *if* + past simple for the unlikely or impossible condition. We use *would* + infinitive without *to* for the result.

   If we lost our way, we would shout for help.

- We can write the two parts of the sentence in any order. When we start with the *if* part, we separate the two parts with a comma.

   If I went to bed at midnight, I would be tired the next day.

- When we start with the result, we don't separate the two halves with a comma.

   I would be happy if Louise agreed to go out with me.

Common mistakes

~~If I would have more money, I'd buy a new bike.~~ ✗
If I had more money, I'd buy a new bike. ✓
~~I wouldn't help you if you wouldn't be my friend.~~ ✗
I wouldn't help you if you weren't my friend. ✓

8b I wish we could stay longer.

Vocabulary: Phrasal verbs with *out, up, on*

1 ★ **Complete the dialogues with one word in each space.**

1 A: Come on Tom. Get _up_.

B: But it's only nine o'clock.

A: Yes, it's breakfast time. I want you to get some milk. We've run _____.

2 A: If you want to find _____ more about Easter Island, you can look it _____ on the internet.

B: It's not easy.

A: All you have to do is turn _____ your computer!

3 A: I feel terrible.

B: Cheer _____, it's Saturday.

A: It doesn't matter. I always feel terrible in the morning since I gave _____ drinking coffee.

2 ★★ **Complete the sentences with the correct form of the phrasal verbs from the box.**

- run out of • ~~give up~~ • cheer up • get up
- turn on • look up • get on with • look out

1 If I _gave up_ eating fast food, I'd feel much healthier.

2 I'd invite John to my party if we _____ each other better.

3 It would be warmer if you _____ the heating.

4 If we _____ petrol here, we'd have to walk a long way.

5 If you went to bed earlier, you'd _____ earlier.

6 If I had a dictionary, I'd _____ this word that I don't understand.

7 If you drove more carefully, I wouldn't shout '_____' every thirty seconds!

8 If the weather was warmer, it would _____ us all _____.

Grammar: *I wish* with past simple

3 ★ **Choose the correct options.**

1 My friends are going to a concert on Friday. I wish I **have / has / had** a ticket.

2 My parents didn't want me to go. I wish they **don't / didn't / won't** worry about me so much.

3 My brother is going. Sometimes I wish I **am / would be / was** a boy!

4 I could go with him, but his friends are annoying. I wish they **weren't / aren't / won't be** so stupid.

5 I could go with my brother then leave him outside and meet my friends but he'd tell my parents. I wish he **wouldn't / wasn't / isn't** so honest.

6 The band are an all female band. I wish I **would be / was / am** in a band.

7 The problem is my voice. I wish I **would / can't / could** sing.

4 ★ **Complete the sentences with the correct form of the verbs in brackets.**

1 I wish the food _was_ (be) better.

2 I wish my parents _____ (not argue) all the time.

3 I wish I _____ (can) windsurf.

4 I wish it _____ (not be) raining.

5 I wish I _____ (have) more money.

6 I wish the hotel _____ (be) nicer.

7 I wish my friends _____ (be) here.

8 I wish I _____ (know) the waitress' name.

5 ⭐⭐ Use the prompts to write sentences.

1 wish/not/my last day

I wish this wasn't my last day.

2 wish/she/can/come to England with us

_____

3 wish/I/speak/better Spanish

_____

4 wish/my friends/can/see me now

_____

5 wish/my parents/be somewhere else

_____

6 wish/knew/somewhere interesting to take her

_____

7 wish/have/cooler clothes

_____

8 wish/this evening/can last forever

_____

6 ⭐⭐⭐ Write wishes for the situations.

1 I'm tired.

I wish I wasn't tired.

2 I can't swim.

_____

3 I have to tidy my room every Saturday.

_____

4 We've got a test tomorrow.

_____

5 I haven't got a job.

_____

6 My friend and I keep arguing.

_____

Grammar summary

I wish with past simple

Affirmative

I **wish** I **had** a brother.

I **wish** I **could** drive.

I **wish** I **knew** more people.

I **wish** I **was** taller.

Negative

I **wish** I **didn't have** so much homework to do.

I **wish** we **didn't live** here.

I **wish** my hair **wasn't** red.

I **wish** I **didn't get** so nervous.

Note

Use

- We use this verb pattern to say how we would like the present to be different to how it is now.
  I wish it wasn't raining. (It's raining.)
  I wish I could speak French. (I can't speak French.)

Form

- We use *I wish* + subject + past simple.
  I wish I was rich.
  I wish you were here.
  I wish I had more time.
  I wish you didn't have to go.

- *Wish* means the situation is unlikely to happen or impossible. When something is possible, we use *I hope* + present simple.
  I wish I could see you tomorrow. (I know it's impossible.)
  I hope I can see you tomorrow. (It's possible.)

Common mistakes

~~I wish I'm not shy.~~ ✗

I wish I wasn't shy. ✓

~~I wish we have more money.~~ ✗

I wish we had more money. ✓

8c It was so boring I fell asleep.

Phrases

1 ★ **Complete the dialogue with the phrases from the box.**

> • What a waste of money • in a minute.
> • ~~No way~~

A: I've got a ticket for Barcelona vs Real Madrid.

B: ¹*No way*! That's amazing. How much did it cost?

A: €100.

C: ² _____. I could do something much more interesting with that amount of money. Do you want me to show you some information about modern jazz concerts in our area?

A: … er, maybe ³ _____. First, I want to see a 3D, 360° view of the Camp Nou stadium from my seat.

B: Can you do that? Wow!

Vocabulary: Types of TV programme

2 ★★ **Complete the sentences with the words from the box.**

> • ~~documentary~~ • news • comedy • quiz
> • Reality TV • wildlife • cookery • talent

1 I saw a very interesting *documentary* about the moon landings last night.

2 Did you see the _____? There was an accident on the motorway this morning.

3 I'm bored with _____ shows. The singers are good but they all sound the same.

4 This is a great _____ programme. I get lots of ideas for meals from it.

5 _____ shows aren't really real. I mean, everyone knows the cameras are watching them.

6 This is a difficult _____ show. Do you know the name of Henry VIII's third wife?

7 I love _____ programmes. This one is about penguins in Antarctica.

8 This is a really funny _____.

Grammar: *so* + adjective … *(that)* …; *such (a/an)* + adjective + noun *(that)* …

3 ★ **Complete the sentences with *so* or *such*.**

1 The singers were *so* good that it was difficult to choose the winner.

2 It was _____ an exciting film that I watched it twice in one night.

3 The advert breaks are _____ long that you can make a cup of tea during them.

4 It was _____ a difficult quiz that two people didn't get any answers right at all.

5 I was watching _____ a stupid cartoon that my mum told me to switch it off.

6 The reality show was _____ unpopular that it only lasted three weeks.

4 ★★ **Complete the text with the phrases from the box.**

> • so old • such a waste • so convinced
> • so disappointing • ~~so realistic~~ • so popular
> • such a powerful • so sad

Cathy Come Home was a television play but it was ¹*so realistic* that people thought it was a documentary. It was about a young couple who lost their jobs, then their home and then their children. It was ² _____ that I cried when I saw it.

The play is ³ _____ that it was made in black and white, but it was ⁴ _____ story that it doesn't matter that it isn't in colour. Why is it still ⁵ _____?

First of all it was different. It also had a big effect on the audience. People were ⁶ _____ that it was real that, when they saw the actress who played Cathy in the street, they often stopped her and tried to give her money.

Cathy Come Home really changed the way people thought. That's why it's

7_____ that all there is on television now is reality TV shows and talent contests. They are 8_____ of time!

Use your English: Make suggestions

5 ⭐ **Match the beginnings (1–9) to the endings (a–i).**

1 Let's
2 How
3 Do
4 We
5 Why
6 Shall
7 That
8 I'd rather
9 I'd prefer

a) not go out today.
b) you fancy having a picnic?
c) we cycle to the forest?
d) not to go jogging.
e) could go shopping.
f) play football.
g) don't we stay at home?
h) about going to a café?
i) sounds good.

6 ⭐⭐ **Complete the dialogues with one word in each space.**

1 A: Hi, Sam. Do you f<u>ancy</u> helping me choose a new game for my computer?

B: Yes, that s_____ good.
L_____'s meet at Maria's Café for a cola first.

A: I don't really fancy cola. How a_____ going to the juice bar?

B: I'm not s_____. It sounds a bit boring.

A: No, it isn't. The drinks are delicious.

B: Oh, OK.

2 A: S_____ we go outside? The sun's shining.

B: I'd r_____ stay here.

A: Why? It's boring here. We could meet Harry.

B: Oh no. I'd p_____ not to meet anyone from school. All they talk about is exams.

A: Well, h_____ about phoning Kerry. You like her, don't you?

B: No, not r_____. I mean, she's OK, but she always wants to play sports. I hate sports.

Grammar summary

so + adjective … (that) …
such (a/an) + adjective + noun (that) …

so + adjective … (that) …

The house was **so dark** that I couldn't see anything.
The test was **so difficult** that the highest mark was 54%.

such (a/an) + adjective + noun (that) …

We had **such a good time** that we are going back to the same place next summer.
It was **such a funny film** that I couldn't stop laughing.

Note

Use

- We use *so* and *such (a/an)* to emphasise adjectives.
  It was cold. It was so cold that I had to wear two sweaters.
- We use *so* + adjective and *such (a/an)* + adjective + noun with *that* to show the result of the situation.
  I was so tired that I went to bed at eight o'clock.
  It was such a loud party that the neighbours complained.

Common mistakes

~~We are so good friends that we go everywhere together.~~ ✗
We are such good friends that we go everywhere together. ✓

1 Use the prompts to write questions and answers.

1 A: you/fancy/meet/on Sunday?

  B: prefer/meet/on Saturday.

A: Do you fancy meeting on Sunday?

B: I'd prefer to meet on Saturday.

2 A: what/you do/you be/on a talent show?

  B: if/I/be/on a talent show/I/sing.

  _____

  _____

3 A: if/you/lose/your phone/you cry?

  B: ✗

  _____

  _____

4 A: What/you wish/you can/do?

  B: wish/can/speak/a foreign language

  _____

  _____

5 A: you wear/a suit/you go/on a date?

  B: ✗./I/wear/jeans

  _____

  _____

.../8

2 Complete the sentences with the correct form of the verbs in brackets.

1 I wish I *could* (can) drive.

2 If I _____ (have) a car, I _____ (drive) you to the beach.

3 If I _____ (speak) German, I _____ (understand) this letter.

4 I'd prefer_____ (not do) anything this evening.

5 If we _____ (not have) any money, we _____ (can't) have a pizza.

6 I wish I _____ (not have) a younger brother.

7 I wish you_____ (not live) so far away.

8 My boyfriend _____ (come) to our house if my parents _____ (like) him.

.../11

3 Complete the dialogue with the words from the box. There are three extra words.

> • would • bored • was • turn on • prefer
> • go on • interesting • stopped • such • find out
> • so • give up • rather • boring • don't • wish

A: When I play sports, I'm ¹*so* slow that nobody wants me on their team.

B: You should ² _____ eating crisps. I read an ³ _____ article about how unhealthy they are. Why ⁴ _____ you bring carrots to school?

A: Good idea. I ⁵ _____ I knew about healthy food like you do.

B: If you ⁶ _____ playing computer games, you ⁷ _____ have time to ⁸ _____ more.

A: I know. I wish I ⁹ _____ better organised. Sometimes I ¹⁰ _____ the computer at eight and, suddenly, it's midnight. It's ¹¹ _____ an exciting game that I can't stop playing.

B: Do you think so? I got ¹² _____ with it after a few minutes. I'd ¹³ _____ play a real sport.

.../12

4 Complete the text with one word in each space.

If you look ¹*up* the word 'soap ² _____' you'll find that the definition is a programme which has a story which ³ _____ on for a long time. We get to know the characters and find ⁴ _____ about their lives. The radio show, *The Archers*, started in 1951 and, ⁵ _____ you wanted to listen to every episode, it ⁶ _____ take about 4,250 hours! My mum thinks it is ⁷ _____ good that she really hates missing it. Dad would prefer ⁸ _____ to listen to it, but he often doesn't have a choice. He's ⁹ _____ a kind man. He never complains. He says that it's a shame Mum doesn't ¹⁰ _____ on as well with our real neighbours.

.../9

🎧 **LISTEN AND CHECK YOUR SCORE**

Total	.../40

8 Skills practice

SKILLS FOCUS: READING, LISTENING AND WRITING

Read

1 Read the text and answer the questions.

1 When was the Maths test?

It was on Monday 10th February.

2 Who cheated in the test?

_____

3 What did Lucy do when she got home?

_____

4 What did the headmaster say Lucy had done wrong?

_____

5 Why did Lucy get a special prize from the headmaster?

_____

It was Monday 10th February and Lucy was sitting in a Maths test with the rest of her class. Suddenly, she noticed two girls passing pieces of paper to each other. When they got their results, the two girls who had cheated, Cathy and Nicola, came top. Lucy came third and she was very upset.

That evening she turned on her computer and wrote a blog. She put a big heading on it: 'Cheats!' and she wrote what had happened. She even wrote the girls' names although she knew that some of their friends read her blog.

The next day at school, no one talked to Lucy and people stared at her as they passed. Then the headmaster asked to see her. He told her that he understood her anger, but that naming the two girls was wrong.

After that, the teachers were much more careful about cheating in exams. In the end of year exams, Lucy came top of the school in Maths and was given a special prize by the headmaster in front of the whole school. Cathy and Nicola failed their Maths exams.

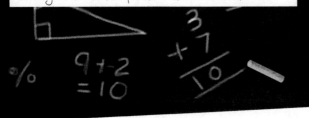

Listen

2 🎧 Listen to the dialogue and tick the things that Laura says.

1 She is going to be on a TV quiz show. ✓

2 She could win a million pounds.

3 She can win something for her school.

4 She'd like to buy some books.

5 Her special subject is Jane Austen.

6 She likes History.

7 She likes playing computer games.

3 🎧 Listen again and choose the correct options.

1 The name of the TV show is ___ *Do You Know*?.

  a) *How*   b) *Who*   c) *What*

2 Laura can win ___ for herself.

  a) books   b) money   c) a laptop

3 Laura gives ___ examples of school subjects that the questions might be about.

  a) two   b) three   c) four

4 If Ian was on the show, he would want to answer questions about ___.

  a) science   b) computer games

  c) Jane Austen

5 Ian likes ___ about the Second World War.

  a) playing games   b) reading   c) learning

Write

4 Use the ideas below to write a blog.

Choose a kind of television programme that you don't like. Write a blog with the title:

Who watches (the type of programme you are writing about)?

• Explain what the type of programme is.

• Explain why you don't like it.

• Choose one programme that is typical of the type and describe it.

• Explain why you think some people do like this type of programme.

9a You can't afford to buy it.

Phrases

1 ⭐ **Complete the dialogues with the phrases from the box.**

• go halves • I'd so like • Nice try
• That's all • ~~I know what you mean~~
---

1 A: Some mobile phones are really expensive.

   B: *I know what you mean.*

2 A: Look at these tablets.

   _____ to have one.

   B: You can't afford to buy anything in here.

   A: I know. I'm just looking.

   _____.

3 A: Can I take you out for a pizza?

   B: OK but you don't have to pay. Let's

   _____ this time.

4 A: When Mum and Dad buy us a computer, we have to share it. You can have it four days a week and I'll have it three days.

   B: Really?

   A: Yes, Friday, Saturday and Sunday.

   B: _____ but no way!

Vocabulary: Computer language

2 ⭐ **Complete the sentences with the words from the box.**

• burn • download • stick • connected
• ~~send~~ • delete
---

1 I'll *send* this email then we can go out.

2 If you don't need these old files anymore, you should _____ them.

3 You can't check for new emails because you aren't _____ to the internet.

4 You can _____ this song from the internet and pay for it by credit card.

5 You can _____ this film onto a DVD or you can save it on a memory _____.

3 ⭐⭐ **Complete the dialogue with one word in each space.**

A: I've got some money, but I'm not sure what to buy.

B: Well, this ¹*smartphone* is good. It's got ²w_____ so you can use the internet in lots of places for free. You can also download ³a_____ for travel, the weather, cinemas … anything really.

A: No, I like my phone. What are these?

B: They're ⁴t_____ – flat computers. They have a ⁵t_____. You just touch it with your finger like this.

A: No, I'm not getting one of them.

B: Well, how about an MP3 ⁶p_____. You can ⁷u_____ about a thousand songs to it.

A: Great. I'll get one.

Grammar: Verb with infinitive or gerund

4 ⭐⭐ **Complete the sentences with the correct form of the verbs in brackets.**

1 Paul agreed *to meet* (meet) us outside the theatre.

2 When do you expect _____ (finish) your work?

3 I admit _____ (borrow) your tablet but I deny _____ (break) it.

4 My parents decided _____ (go) camping this year.

5 Keep _____ (try) to connect.

6 I suggest _____ (buy) the more expensive tablet.

7 How do you manage _____ (save) money if you don't work?

8 Stop _____ (waste) my time with your stupid email jokes!

9 Paul offered _____ (help) me install a new antivirus programme.

5 ★★ Choose the correct options.

Jason: I ¹**want** / **fancy** / **suggest** to earn some money for a tablet but I can't find a job.

Sally: Well, ²**manage** / **keep** / **promise** trying. I'm sure you'll get one in the end.

Jason: I don't know. My uncle ³**suggested** / **offered** / **didn't mind** to give me a job, but I don't ⁴**want** / **hope** / **fancy** working for him. He can be quite difficult!

Sally: Well, I ⁵**decide** / **agree** / **suggest** looking on the internet. Jobsite always ⁶**keeps** / **seems** / **admits** to have a lot of local jobs.

Jason: Great. Thanks. I'll have a look later.

6 ★★ Complete the letter with the correct form of the verbs from the box.

• see • study • ~~read~~ • live • change
• write • find • play

Dear Simon,

Thanks for your letter. I enjoyed ¹<u>reading</u> it. I know I promised ²_____ a longer letter this time, but I'm really busy at the moment. I've got a piano concert next week. I can't stand ³_____ the piano, but my mum says I can't give up until the summer and she refuses ⁴_____ her mind. I also go to French classes after school. I don't mind ⁵_____ French because I love France and I hope ⁶_____ there one day if I can manage ⁷_____ a job.

Well, I must go. I look forward to ⁸_____ you in the summer.

Annabella.

Grammar summary

Verb with infinitive

I **want to stay** in bed.
I've **decided to work** harder.
It **seems to be working** now.
She's **promised to help** me.
They **refuse to be** quiet.
Verbs which can be followed by the infinitive include:
afford, agree, decide, expect, hope, manage, offer, promise, refuse, seem, want

Verb with gerund

I **can't stand losing**.
They **enjoy playing** tennis.
We **avoid getting** into trouble.
He **gave up drinking** coffee.
I **look forward to seeing** you soon.
Verbs which can be followed by the gerund include:
admit, avoid, can't stand, deny, enjoy, fancy, finish, give up, keep, look forward to, not mind, miss, practise, stop, suggest

Note

Use

• We follow certain verbs with either the gerund or the infinitive.
  I want to leave. I enjoy swimming.

• We can follow some verbs with either the gerund or the infinitive. These verbs include *hate, love, like, prefer, start.*
  I like walking.
  I like to walk.

• We usually avoid having two *-ing* forms close together.
  I'm starting to enjoy this. NOT ~~I'm starting enjoying this.~~

Common mistakes

~~I look forward to see you soon.~~ ✗
I look forward to seeing you soon. ✓
~~I didn't manage finishing the exam.~~ ✗
I didn't manage to finish the exam. ✓

9b He had to swim on his back.

Vocabulary: Sports (equipment, people and actions)

1 ⭐ **Label the pictures and complete the sentences.**

1 p_layer_

2 c_____

3 s_____

4 u_____

5 n_____

6 r_____

7 The players are h_____ the ball.

8 g_____

9 g_____

10 r_____

11 p_____

12 The players are k_____ the ball.

13 b_____

14 h_____

15 g_____

16 p_____

17 The player is t_____ the ball.

2 ⭐ **Choose the correct options.**

1 A goalkeeper in football usually wears ___.

   a) helmet   b) gloves

2 Tennis players hit the ball with a ___.

   a) bat   b) racket

3 The person who controls a football match is the ___.

   a) referee   b) umpire

4 In basketball, you score ___.

   a) points   b) runs

5 You can draw, lose or ___ a match.

   a) beat   b) win

6 You can draw with, lose to or ___ another player or team.

   a) beat   b) win

3 ⭐⭐ **Complete the texts with one of the words in capitals in each space. There are three extra words for each text.**

~~POINTS~~/GOALS/MATCH/KICK/BASKET/ THROWS/NET/TEAMS/PASS

Here we are at the basketball stadium. The score is 32 [1]_points_ to 28 so it's an exciting [2]_____. These are two of the best [3]_____ in the country and there's a big crowd to see them. Now, Murphy has the ball, he and Jessup [4]_____ it to each other and Murphy runs and [5]_____ it high into the air and it's in the [6]_____. That makes it 32–30.

LOSE/GOALKEEPERS/WIN/GOALS /PLAYERS/ DRAW/BEAT

The match between Manchester United and Liverpool has ended in a 0–0 [7]_____ so there were no [8]_____ for the spectators to enjoy. The two [9]_____ were excellent and no-one could get the ball past them. Now, Manchester must [10]_____ Chelsea in their last match to become champions again. Can they do it?

Grammar: Rules and obligation: *must* and *have to*

4 ⭐ **Complete the dialogue with the phrases from the box.**

- have to keep   • mustn't throw
- mustn't bowl   • ~~have to run~~   • have to throw
- don't have to bowl   • don't have to run
- have to run

A: What are the main differences between baseball and cricket?

B: Well, in baseball, if they hit the ball, they ¹*have to run*. In cricket you ²_____ at all. You can stay there all day if you want.

A: What about the people who throw the ball?

B: Well, in baseball they ³_____ the ball in a certain place. They ⁴_____ it behind the batsman or very low or very high. In cricket, we don't say throw, we say bowl. You ⁵_____ the ball in the same place all the time. Of course, you ⁶_____ it straight at the batsman's head!

A: No, of course not. So, is bowling like throwing?

B: Not exactly. You ⁷_____ your arm straight when you bowl. When you throw it, you bend it at the elbow. If you want to bowl it fast, you ⁸_____ before you bowl it.

A: Oh, OK. Thanks.

5 ⭐⭐ **Complete the sentences with the correct form of *have to* or *mustn't*.**

1 I *had to* stay at school yesterday and write 'I _____ talk while the teacher is talking' 100 times.

2 I got home early yesterday. I _____ wait for the bus because my friend's mum gave me a lift in her car.

3 My dad gets sports tickets free from work. He _____ buy them, but he _____ sell them or he could lose his job. When he started the job he _____ promise never to sell them.

Grammar summary

Rules and obligation: *must* and *have to*

Obligation
Present
We **must finish** this project soon.
You **have to be** at the training session by six o'clock.
He **has to wear** a helmet
I **mustn't be** late.
Past
They **had to leave** before the end of the match.
No obligation
Present
You **don't have to do** the washing-up.
She **doesn't have to go** to bed early.
Past
We **didn't have to pay** for anything.

Note

Use

- We usually use *must* to talk about obligations that come from the speaker.
  I must get my hair cut. (It looks a mess.)
- We usually use *have to* to talk about obligations from other people.
  I have to get my hair cut. (My parents told me to.)
- We use *mustn't* for negative obligations from the speaker or from other people.
  I mustn't forget my phone. (My rules.)
  You mustn't drive at more than 50 kph. (It's the law.)
- The past form of *must* and *have to* is *had to*.
  I had to go home at nine o'clock.
- We use *don't have to* when there is no obligation. The third person singular form of *don't have to* is *doesn't have to* and the past form is *didn't have to*.
  We don't have to wear a uniform at my new school.
  She doesn't have to make her bed.
  We didn't have to do homework at our old school.

Form

- We use the correct form of *must* or *have to* + the infinitive without *to*.

9c It's so different from London.

Grammar and vocabulary:
Adjectives with prepositions

1 ⭐ **Match the beginnings (1–10) to the endings (a–j).**

1 We're very proud   _e_

2 Berlin is famous   ___

3 My parents were angry   ___

4 We were all very surprised   ___

5 The buildings in Riga are similar   ___

6 If you're interested   ___

7 Sonia is getting very worried   ___

8 I was really impressed   ___

9 I'm not keen   ___

10 The film is very different   ___

a) to the ones in St Petersburg.

b) with me for being late home.

c) about her exams.

d) on fish.

e) of you for doing so well in your exams.

f) at Bill's behaviour.

g) by your speech to the rest of the school.

h) from the book.

i) for a wall that doesn't exist now.

j) in books, why don't you join the library?

2 ⭐⭐ **Choose the correct options.**

1 I'm not responsible ___ my brother's mess!

    a) for   b) from   c) with

2 I can't play basketball. I'm really bad ___ it.

    a) with   b) of   c) at

3 I'm fed up ___ all your questions.

    a) about   b) with   c) from

4 I'm so tired ___ your silly jokes!

    a) with   b) about   c) of

5 Are you getting excited ___ your holiday?

    a) in   b) of   c) about

6 My new phone is very different ___ my old one.

    a) from   b) with   c) of

7 Mr Phillips was really impressed ___ our project.

    a) in   b) by   c) of

3 ⭐⭐ **Complete the dialogues with the correct prepositions.**

1 A: What subjects are you good _at_?

  B: I'm not very good _at_ anything!

2 A: Why are you annoyed ___ your brother?

  B: I'm fed up ___ him borrowing my phone.

3 A: What are you scared ___?

  B: I'm really frightened ___ heights.

4 A: What are you interested ___?

  B: I'm interested ___ music and dance.

5 A: Were you impressed ___ anything in Germany?

  B: I was very impressed ___ the clean streets.

6 A: What did you think of Krakow?

  B: I loved it. It was similar ___ Prague. It was very different ___ how I had imagined it.

7 A: What sports do you like?

  B: Well, I'm keen ___ rugby, but I get bored ___ athletics.

4 ⭐⭐⭐ **Complete the dialogue with the adjectives from the box.**

> • keen • impressed • good • famous
> • similar • ~~bored~~ • interested • scared

A: I'm ¹_bored_ with these computer games. Let's do something else.

B: OK. We could play tennis.

A: I'm not very ²_____ at tennis. In fact I'm not ³_____ on sports at all.

B: So what are you ⁴_____ in?

A: I love films.

B: OK. Let's go to the cinema. There's a good horror film on. Are you ⁵_____ of horror films?

A: A little bit but I love them!

.....

A: That was great. I was really ⁶_____ by the special effects.

B: Yes, but it wasn't a new story. It was very ⁷_____ to a lot of films I've seen.

A: Well, the director is ⁸_____ for using other people's ideas, but he's brilliant.

Use your English: Say goodbye

5 ★ **Choose the correct options.**

1 A: I'm going to Italy tomorrow.

   B: Have a good trip. / Take a trip.

2 A: We're going skiing next week.

   B: **Take care. / Safe care.**

3 A: Bye, Mum. Bye, Dad.

   B: Bye. **Look / Take** after yourself.

4 A: See you soon.

   B: **I hope so. / I hope too.**

5 A: See you in September.

   B: Yes. **Keep / Call** in touch.

6 A: **Let us know / Have a safe trip** when you get there.

   B: I will.

7 A: Don't forget to call.

   B: **I don't. / I won't.**

6 ★★ **Complete the dialogue with the words from the box.**

• care • soon • won't • ~~have~~ • know
• touch • great • trip • after • will • forget

Amy: I'm really excited about my holiday.

Harry: I'm not surprised. ¹*Have* a safe
      ² _____.

Amy: Thanks.

Harry: And have a ³_____ time.

Amy: I ⁴_____.

Harry: Take ⁵_____ on your bike.

Amy: Don't worry.

Harry: And look ⁶_____ yourself. Don't
      ⁷_____ to keep in ⁸_____.

Amy: I ⁹_____.

Harry: Let me ¹⁰_____ when you get to the ferry.

Amy: OK, I will.

Harry: And I'll see you ¹¹_____.

Amy: Yes, see you in three weeks.

Grammar summary

Adjectives with prepositions

Alan's **good at** swimming.
I'm **fed up with** this weather.
Are you **scared of** flying?
You're very **similar to** your brother.
I'm **worried about** the future.
Are you **interested in** computers?
I wasn't very **impressed by** the paintings.
This band are **different from** most bands.
Who's **responsible for** these children?
I'm not very **keen on** discos.

Note

Use

• There are many adjectives which we collocate with prepositions. These include:

   – good, bad, surprised   + at
   – fed up, bored, angry, annoyed + with
   – similar   + to
   – excited, upset, worried   + about
   – interested   + in
   – impressed   + by
   – different   + from
   – famous, responsible   + for
   – keen   + on

Form

• We can follow the preposition with a noun or a verb. When we follow the preposition with a verb, we use the gerund form (-ing).

   I'm interested in visiting the museum.
   He's worried about taking his driving test.
   We're keen on singing.

Common mistakes

~~I'm interested for history.~~ ✗
I'm interested in history. ✓
~~I'm excited about reach the age of eighteen.~~ ✗
I'm excited about reaching the age of eighteen. ✓

1 Complete the sentences with one word in each space.

1 Footballers *kick* the ball.

2 Wear p_____ on your legs and arms to protect them.

3 You s_____ people emails.

4 Footballers try to s_____ a goal.

5 You play football on a p_____.

6 Remember to c_____ the battery in your phone.

7 In basketball, you t_____ the ball into the basket.

8 You r_____ a computer by switching it off and then on again.

.../14

2 Complete the second sentence so that it has the same meaning as the first.

1 It is against the law to camp here.
You *mustn't camp here*.

2 The tickets were free.
We _____ pay for the tickets.

3 My parents told me to do the washing-up last night.
I _____ the washing-up last night.

4 I'm not going to eat meat!
John refused _____ meat.

5 I really hate playing rugby.
I can't _____ rugby.

6 I've stopped going to dance lessons.
I've given _____ to dance lessons.

7 Sam said that he hadn't broken the window.
Sam denied _____ window.

8 Alison said that she would come to my party.
Alison agreed _____ my party.

.../7

3 Complete the sentences with the words from the box. There are three extra words.

• ~~athletes~~ • with • about • won • online • internet • to • team • for

1 In the first Olympic Games, there were no female [1]*athletes*.

2 I've been chosen for the school basketball _____.

3 Do you have _____ do any exercise after school?

4 I'm responsible _____ putting the pads back after cricket practice.

5 My dad is worried _____ his health.

6 I watch football matches _____.

.../10

4 Choose the correct options.

My dad organises a children's basketball [1](team)/ match / player. He [2]mustn't / had to / doesn't have to – he just enjoys doing it. He can't [3]stand / mind / like losing and he worries a lot [4]for / about / with the matches the team plays. He gives long talks to his team about the best way to [5]win / beat / score their match. He forgets that the players are only ten years old!

My mum has tried to make him give up [6]run / to run / running the team and doesn't want him to be the [7]umpire / coach / referee anymore, but dad refuses [8]listen / to listen / listening to her. He really looks forward [9]watching / to watch / to watching the matches and would really miss it if he gave up. Mum even went to our doctor for his advice, but he told her that she [10]mustn't / has to / had to worry and that it was probably making my dad healthier than if he sat around the house doing nothing all day.

.../9

🎧 **LISTEN AND CHECK YOUR SCORE**

Total	.../40

9 Skills practice

SKILLS FOCUS: READING AND WRITING

Read

1 **Read the text and complete the sentences with A (Charlie), B (Michelle) or C (Luis).**

1 _A_ has made an album.

2 ___ doesn't use his/her real name.

3 ___ has made films for television.

4 ___ has appeared in newspapers.

5 ___ works for a famous company.

6 ___ has asked people to suggest ideas.

Over 1,000 people now earn $100,000 or more from YouTube. Here are some of the most popular.

A Charlie McDonnell.
Charlie set up his own YouTube channel, Charlieissocoollike, in 2007. He had the idea of 'challenge Charlie'. People could send him ideas of what to do in his videos. One was a dance from a Hannah Montana film. Charlie has also made an album of songs, an idea fans suggested after seeing him singing on his videos.

B Michelle Phan
When Michelle was five years old, she was invited to a Halloween party. Her parents didn't have enough money for a costume so Michelle used whatever she could find and went as a lion. Now, millions of people watch her videos on beauty advice. Michelle has appeared in several magazines and newspapers and, in 2009, she started working for the French company Lancôme, whose products she now sometimes uses in her videos.

C Luis Cruikshank
Luis is an American actor but in his videos, he plays Fred Figglehorn, a six-year-old boy. These hilarious videos were, at one time, the most popular on YouTube. Not surprisingly, a TV channel decided to make a series of full-length Fred movies. A lot of people watched the films, but the YouTube videos are much funnier.

Write

2 **Connect the sentences with _although_ and _however_.**

1 I'd like a smartphone. I'm not sure they are worth the money.
   Although I'd like a smartphone, I'm not sure
   they are worth the money.
   I'd like a smartphone. However, I'm not sure
   they are worth the money.

2 I spend a lot of time on the internet. I don't send any emails.
   _____
   _____

3 I love watching football on the TV. I don't like playing it.
   _____
   _____

3 **Complete the text about school sports with _although_ or _however_.**

[1]_Although_ there is a good choice of sports for students to play, the school doesn't have a cricket pitch. In my opinion, this would be a useful thing for the school to have. [2]_____, I realise that it would be expensive and couldn't be used in bad weather.

The most popular sport in the school is football, [3]_____ the school's team aren't very good. They lost their first eight matches, [4]_____ they have done better recently.

The least popular sport is rugby. [5]_____, the students in the school team are very keen. Other students don't want to play, because they feel unwanted. [6]_____, Mr Elkins, the rugby coach, always tries to help the weaker players.

4 **Write a similar report on computers in your school.**

Although there are a lot of computers/only a few computers in our school …

Pearson Education Limited
Edinburgh Gate
Harlow
Essex CM20 2JE
England
and Associated Companies throughout the world.

www.english.com/livebeat

First published 2015

ISBN: 978-1-4479-5288-6

Tenth impression 2023

Set in Helvetica Neue LT Std 55 Roman 10/14pt

Printed and bound by CPI Group (UK) Ltd, Croydon, CR0 4YY

Illustration Acknowledgements

(Key: b-bottom; c-centre; l-left; r-right; t-top)

Kathy Baxendale 5, 7t, 8, 25; Robin Lawrie (Beehive Illustration) 59, 60, 74; Sean Longcroft 17, 32, 53, 57, 66, 67; Pat Murray (Graham-Cameron Illustrations) 73; Eric Smith 7b, 10, 18, 24, 34, 42, 65, 76; James Walmesley (Graham-Cameron Illustrations) 6, 16, 40, 44, 48.

Photo Acknowledgements

The publisher would like to thank the following for their kind permission to reproduce their photographs:

(Key: b-bottom; c-centre; l-left; r-right; t-top)

Alamy Images: City Image 31tr, imagebroker 9, Kumar Sriskandan 31/3; **DK Images:** Neil Setchfield 21/7, Jules Selmes 21/3; **Fotolia. com:** boscorelli 63, Irena Lavrenteva 41, Richard Villalon 43; **John Foxx Images:** Images 4 Communication 31/1; **Rex Features:** Billy Farrell Agency 21/5, David Fisher 21/1; **Shutterstock.com:** Alan Freed 31/2, Gail Johnson 47

All other images © Pearson Education

Cover images: *Front*: **Shutterstock.com:** Rido

Every effort has been made to trace the copyright holders and we apologise in advance for any unintentional omissions. We would be pleased to insert the appropriate acknowledgement in any subsequent edition of this publication.